FROM THE BIBLE-TEACHING MINISTRY OF
CHARLES R. SWINDOLL

GROWING DEEP
IN THE
CHRISTIAN
LIFE

• *Returning to Our Roots* •

INSIGHT FOR LIVING
INSIGHTS AND APPLICATION WORKBOOK

INSIGHT FOR LIVING

GROWING DEEP IN THE CHRISTIAN LIFE
Returning to Our Roots

Charles R. Swindoll has devoted his life to the clear, practical teaching and application of God's Word and His grace. A pastor at heart, Chuck has served as senior pastor to congregations in Texas, Massachusetts, and California. He currently is the senior pastor of Stonebriar Community Church in Frisco, Texas, but Chuck's listening audience extends far beyond a local church body. As a leading program in Christian broadcasting, *Insight for Living* airs in major Christian radio markets around the world, reaching people groups in languages they can understand. Chuck's extensive writing ministry has also served the body of Christ worldwide and his leadership as president and now chancellor of Dallas Theological Seminary has helped prepare and equip a new generation for ministry. Chuck and Cynthia, his partner in life and ministry, have four grown children and ten grandchildren.

Based upon the original outlines, charts, and transcripts of Charles R. Swindoll's sermons, the workbook text was developed and written by Marla Alupoaicei, a creative writer in the Creative Ministries Department of Insight for Living. Marla is a graduate of Dallas Theological Seminary with the Master of Theology degree.

Editor in Chief: Cynthia Swindoll, President, Insight for Living
Director: Mark Gaither, Th.M., Dallas Theological Seminary
Theological Editor: Wayne Stiles, Th.M., D.Min., Dallas Theological Seminary
Research Assistant: Michael Kibbe, B.A., Biblical Studies, Cedarville University
Content Editors: Amy Snedaker, B.A., English, Rhodes College
        Brie Engeler, B.A., University Scholars, Baylor University
Collaborative material was provided by the Creative Ministries Department.
Copy Editors: Jim Craft, Cari Harris, Mike Penn
Cover Designer: Joe Casas
Production artist: Nancy Gallaher

Published by IFL Publishing House, A Division of Insight for Living
Post Office Box 251007, Plano, Texas 75025-1007

ISBN 1-57972-586-4
Printed in the United States of America

CONTENTS

A LETTER FROM CHUCK

When you hear the term *theology*, what images come to mind? People arguing over what the Bible says about a particular issue? Preachers giving boring sermons using big words that no one understands? Scholars in their ivory towers, discussing so many confusing terms and "-ologies" that your head starts to spin?

You may be surprised to learn that, in fact, *theology* simply means "the study of God." Rather than being an irrelevant and dull endeavor, digging deeper into theology should be a delight for us. Why? Because it reveals the person of God and the ways He has made Himself known to us through His Word and through His Son, Jesus Christ. Let's strip away all the fear of theology, forget all the long terms that none of us can pronounce, and get back to the basics of knowing our loving and gracious God as we search out the main doctrines and discover the deep truths of His Word.

In this workbook, we'll address eleven key doctrines of the Christian faith and discover how they apply practically to our everyday lives. We'll also find out how these doctrines developed and how studying them can equip us to meet the challenges of our twenty-first century, postmodern culture. By digging deeper into these eleven essentials of the faith, we'll find ourselves better equipped to live the wise, abundant, victorious lives that God designed for us to live.

In this workbook, as you learn more about these doctrines, you'll also have the opportunity to answer specific questions that will help you evaluate your own spiritual life. Your understanding of Scripture will grow as you consider your commitment to the church, address your struggles and weaknesses honestly, and pinpoint your particular gifts and strengths. You'll also learn how to apply the principles of God's Word and the doctrines of your faith to the sticky situations you face virtually every day.

We've added a special question-and-answer feature to this workbook called "In Case You Were Wondering." One of these features appears in each chapter. In total, these features answer twenty-two of the most pressing questions that our readers and listeners continue to ask about theology, the church, and practical issues related to living the spiritual life. We hope these sections will help you come to terms with tough issues as you connect them to your immediate personal experiences. No doubt, you'll want to share these truths with friends, family members, and church members who may be struggling with a particular issue.

We're so glad that you decided to join us on this journey of discovery. Now, plant yourself in a great place for reading as we prepare to grow deep!

Charles R. Swindoll

HOW TO USE THIS WORKBOOK

The goal of this workbook is simple: to provide you with encouragement, biblical principles, application, and practical insights that will help you to grow deeper in your personal relationship with God. This workbook will serve as an ideal tool for your personal devotions, small-group Bible studies, and church curriculum.

Personal Devotions—When your one-on-one time with God needs direction, this Insights and Application workbook will guide you on the path toward greater wisdom, knowledge, and spiritual maturity.

Small-Group Bible Studies—When your small group desires to lay biblical foundations and build authentic community, this workbook will provide your group with a blueprint for learning God's Word and encouraging each other as you live together under His construction.

Church Curriculum—When your church body needs a resource that offers real answers to tough questions, this workbook will provide biblical truth, straight answers, and life-application questions in an exciting, conversation-stimulating format.

You'll find four special features in each chapter of this workbook. These features will help you further unpack the intricacies of Scripture and grow deeper in your spiritual walk with the Almighty.

 Group Discussion Questions—These questions are geared specifically to stimulate lively, thoughtful small-group discussion, though you'll also find them applicable and valuable to your individual study.

Getting to the Root — In this section, you'll learn the origins and meanings of Hebrew and Greek words from the original biblical text. You'll also discover how to better understand and apply specific scriptural terms.

 Digging Deeper — In this section, you'll have the opportunity for personal reflection, deep soul-searching, and spiritual application as you glean principles from God's Word and the workbook chapter and integrate them into your life.

 In Case You Were Wondering — This question-and-answer feature will address some tough theological questions and issues that often arise in the church today. It will also help you to understand how each issue influences your spiritual walk.

Our prayer is that the biblical principles and applications you glean from this workbook will revolutionize your spiritual life. As you incorporate what you've learned and grow deeper in your wisdom and knowledge of God and His Word, you'll gain greater spiritual maturity and confidence.

GROWING DEEP
IN THE
CHRISTIAN
LIFE

• *Returning to Our Roots* •

DOCTRINE AND DISCERNMENT

1

THE VALUE OF KNOWING THE SCOOP

1 Timothy 4:1–6

A college professor named Jaime O'Neill proved the value of knowing the scoop.

O'Neill had grown increasingly concerned about the lack of knowledge among the university students in his classroom, so he devised an eighty-six-question general knowledge quiz and gave it to his English class. He did this not to take pot shots at their ignorance, but to reveal to them their lack of proficiency in real-life knowledge. The questions were not technical or tricky in nature; they were simple questions about aspects of geography, history, famous people, and other areas of basic knowledge.

O'Neill's class had twenty-six students, ranging in age from eighteen to fifty-four. The results of his study were so startling that the professor published them in *Newsweek* magazine in an article titled "No Allusions in the Classroom." Here's a sampling of what he found:

> Ralph Nader is a baseball player. Charles Darwin invented gravity. Christ was born in the 16th century. . . . "The Great Gatsby" was a magician in the 1930s. Franz Joseph Haydn was a songwriter during the same decade. Sid Caesar was an early Roman emperor. Mark Twain invented the cotton gin. Heinrich Himmler invented the Heimlich maneuver. Jefferson Davis was a guitar player for The Jefferson Airplane. Benito Mussolini was a Russian leader of the 18th century.[1]

Shocking, isn't it? What we think of as common knowledge isn't necessarily so common. But we can be sure of this: we can't afford to be culturally illiterate. We can't allow ourselves to become a society that knows so little about history, politics, art, geography, science, technology, and so many other fields that are vitally important to our culture and our daily lives.

Yet perhaps the saddest phenomenon of our day is not the level of cultural illiteracy in our society; it's the prevalence of *biblical* illiteracy. Some of us remain relatively ignorant about the Bible and its spiritual principles and practices. We can't afford to stay that way!

Three Reasons Why We Need to Know the Scoop

Let's examine three reasons why we need to know the scoop when it comes to God's Word.

Ignorance Is Not Bliss

When people are culturally and spiritual ignorant, it shows. Their lack of knowledge provides a fertile breeding ground for prejudice, fear, and superstition. Uneducated people face disadvantages that well-educated people don't face. Nations without a focus on education often end up at the mercy of those nations that place a greater emphasis on knowledge and truth.

Where do you stand with regard to your education and cultural knowledge? More important, how much spiritual and biblical knowledge do you possess? If someone were to give you an eighty-six question quiz about Scripture and the basic doctrines of the Christian faith, how would you score? If a group of Muslims, Mormons, or Jehovah's Witnesses knocked on your door to talk to you about their religion, would you know how to answer their arguments, share Scripture with them, and effectively articulate your personal faith?

Most of us probably wouldn't perform well when faced with tests like these. But if you *do* fall into this category, take heart! We've tailored this study specifically to you. Throughout this workbook, allow these words of the apostle Peter to challenge you to reach a deeper level of biblical knowledge:

> Sanctify Christ as Lord in your hearts, *always being ready to make a defense to everyone who asks you to give an account for the hope that is in you*, yet with gentleness and reverence; and keep a good conscience so that in the thing in which you are slandered, those who revile your good behavior in Christ will be put to shame. (1 Peter 3:15–16, emphasis added)

We're called to always be ready to offer a defense so that we can give an account for the hope that we have through our faith in Christ. That's why ignorance is not bliss! Without a strong understanding of biblical knowledge, we aren't equipped to share the gospel in a way that makes sense and makes others want to know more about our God.

Getting to the Root

The phrase translated "to make a defense" in 1 Peter 3:15 comes from the Greek term *apologia*. The English word *apology* is derived from this term. In Greek, this word does not mean "to apologize" in the sense of telling someone that you're sorry for something you've said or done. Rather, it means "a speech in defense; vindication."[2]

On a scale of 1 to 10, how would you rate your current level of biblical knowledge?

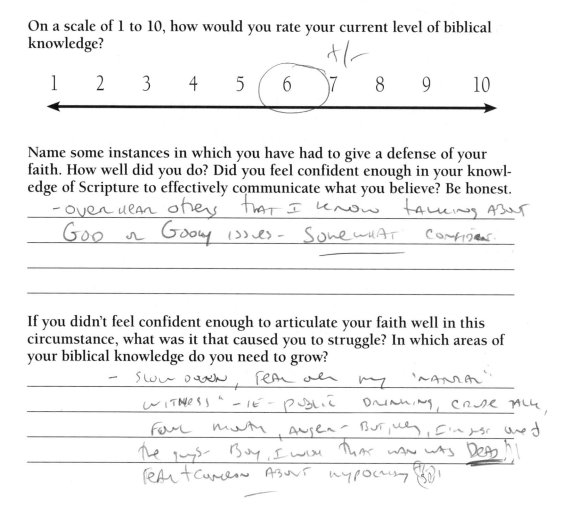

1   2   3   4   5   ⑥   7   8   9   10

Name some instances in which you have had to give a defense of your faith. How well did you do? Did you feel confident enough in your knowledge of Scripture to effectively communicate what you believe? Be honest.

- over hear others that I know talking about God or Goddy issues - Somewhat confident.

If you didn't feel confident enough to articulate your faith well in this circumstance, what was it that caused you to struggle? In which areas of your biblical knowledge do you need to grow?

- Slow down, fear over my "manner"/witness" - ie - public drinking, curse talk, foul mouth, anger - But, yes, I'm just used the guys- Boy, I wish that man was Dead!! Fear + concern about hypocrisy (!)

Now, list several people you know who need to hear the gospel. Take some time to pray, as you continue to learn more about Scripture through this study, that God will provide you with opportunities to share your faith with these people.

> — PAT + CHARLIE
> — LIM, JIM, MEGAN, CARRIE
> — GRANT + DICK, AND MANY —
> — ERIC — AMY & ELSE — JED, RUB.

Knowledge Is Emphasized in Scripture

Throughout Scripture, we're reminded time and again of the importance of our search for knowledge.

- Before the people marched into the land of Canaan, Moses pulled the Israelites aside for a final review of God's Law. Moses exhorted fathers and mothers to teach their children in God's truth—His instructions for living. Why was instilling this knowledge so important? Because the children would soon be exposed to a new lifestyle that would challenge their faith in Yahweh. The Israelites would be moving into a land characterized by idolatry, polygamy, prostitution, and other pagan rituals. So Moses charged these parents ahead of time, "Make sure your children know the truth so they won't be led astray!" (See Deuteronomy 6.)

- In 1 Samuel 2:3, Hannah proclaimed, "The Lord is a God of knowledge." God possesses all knowledge and wisdom, and He created us in His image. Therefore, we too are called to seek knowledge.

- In Colossians 2:3, Paul reminded us that "In whom [Christ] are hidden all the treasures of wisdom and knowledge."

- The apostle Peter exhorted, "Be on your guard so that you are not carried away by the error of unprincipled men and fall from your own steadfastness, but grow in the grace and knowledge of our Lord and Savior Jesus Christ" (2 Peter 3:17–18).

Clearly, God wants us to pursue spiritual knowledge passionately and wholeheartedly. In what ways or avenues (classes, Bible studies, small groups, personal study, journaling, prayer, worship, etc.) are you currently pursuing spiritual knowledge? What opportunities would you like to pursue, either individually or corporately, to help you increase your knowledge?

– This study. (maybe some others); I have potentially [illegible] many books:: personal study - something in Daytimer; journal, prayer, Sunday church – [illegible] Tracey!!!

Sound Doctrine Is Invaluable

Paul issued an exhortation to his young protégé, Timothy, regarding the extreme importance of sound doctrine, ending with:

> But the Spirit explicitly says that in later times some will fall away from the faith, paying attention to deceitful spirits and doctrines of demons, by means of the hypocrisy of liars seared in their own conscience as with a branding iron, men who forbid marriage and advocate abstaining from foods which God has created to be gratefully shared in by those who believe and know the truth. For everything created by God is good, and nothing is to be rejected if it is received with gratitude; for it is sanctified by means of the word of God and prayer.
>
> In pointing out these things to the brethren, you will be a good servant of Christ Jesus, constantly nourished on the words of the faith and of the sound doctrine which you have been following. (1 Timothy 4:1–6)

According to this passage, what types of messages can cause people to fall away from the faith?

– Frustrating the good "drives" (i.e. sex) that God endowed.
– Occultic junk preoccupation c feminism, new-age touchy-feely → garbage – newest junk on the market – name-it-claim-it / faith movement e.g. prophecy [illegible]

According to verse 6, when pointing out these things to the men and women of God, what positive result would Timothy gain? How can you apply this truth to your own life?

- Sureness of his own faith
- Favor from God
- good harvest.
- pray that I will pray & that my
  witness will be stronger of Him.

In Case You Were Wondering

Q: Practically, why do I need to know God's Word and understand biblical doctrine? How will this knowledge influence my day-to-day life?

A: We need to know God's Word and its doctrines because Scripture is the absolute moral standard or "measuring rod" by which we are to live our lives and base our decisions. Paul instructed Timothy further, saying, "All Scripture is God-breathed and is useful for teaching, rebuking, correcting and training in righteousness, so that the man of God may be thoroughly equipped for every good work" (2 Timothy 3:16–17 NIV).

The phrase "God-breathed" is the modern translation of the Greek word *theopneustos*. It's an unusual and powerful figure of speech—a compound of the words *theo* (God) and *pneustor* (breathed). Used only here in the entire New Testament, it tells us that all Scripture originates with God Himself, and consequently bears the stamp of divine origin and ultimate authority. This Book of all books owes its existence to the direct creative work of God Himself, and it's useful for guiding, convicting, correcting, and teaching us to walk in righteousness as we live our daily lives in light of its truth.

Digging Deeper

Warning: Knowledge Alone Can Be Dangerous

Knowledge alone can pose a danger to our spiritual well-being when

. . . it lacks scriptural support.

God's Word should serve as the foundation of truth for our spiritual lives. Any knowledge that we gain must be compared to the wisdom of Scripture. We can be fully confident that any philosophy, idea, behavior, or act that contradicts Scripture is *not* from God. Are you making an effort to view your attitudes and actions through the grid of Scripture?

. . . it becomes an end in itself.

Seeking knowledge simply for knowledge's sake can quickly make us overflow with boastful, arrogant pride. God's Word warns us that in some instances, "Knowledge makes arrogant, but love edifies" (1 Corinthians 8:1). Are you seeking knowledge in order to increase your faith and to edify others in the body of Christ?

. . . it isn't balanced by love and grace.

This world contains many knowledgeable people who don't show love and grace to others. Many churches brim with legalistic believers who use their knowledge to tear people down instead of lifting them up. This kind of knowledge results in an intolerant spirit and a mind-set of exclusivity. Are you intolerant, or do you use your spiritual knowledge in the proper context, demonstrating God's grace to others?

. . . it remains theoretical; when it isn't combined with discernment and action.

Our spiritual knowledge does us no good unless we put it into practice. Are you faithfully living out what you know to be true scripturally? Are you actively applying what you've learned?

From your own experience, list at least one example of a situation in which knowledge alone was dangerous, and describe why.

— Tearing down a contemporary book —
leaving no answer / hope within

How can you balance your knowledge with love and grace when you share the truth with others?

prayer — why are you withering in
the firstplace? people need help to
no go to when — They need nearer
—empathy... God loves all of them!!

SIX BENEFITS OF BEING SPIRITUALLY INFORMED

Why must we be so knowledgeable and well-grounded in the Word of God? Isn't that the responsibility of pastors and missionaries? Yes, but it's our responsibility too. Consider these six reasons why it's essential that all believers be spiritually informed.

Knowledge Gives Substance to Faith

Without the Word of God to provide the basis of our faith, what do we have to rely on? Our own emotions and feelings? Another person's opinions? Some other book? Different religious traditions or rituals? None of these provide a reliable basis for truth. Those who depend on the knowledge and false wisdom of the world will soon realize that they've built their house on the sand. When life's raging storms blow, every house built on sand will be washed from its weak foundation and destroyed (see Matthew 7:26–27).

Knowledge Stabilizes Us during Times of Testing

When we root our lives in the deep, fertile soil of God's Word, we don't have to worry about being uprooted when (not if) trials come. Our spiritual knowledge will stabilize us and equip us to handle all the tests that life sends our way.

Knowledge Enables Us to Handle the Bible Accurately

By knowing the doctrines, flow, and general outline of God's Word, we gain confidence in using our Bible and sharing the Scriptures with others.

Knowledge Equips Us to Detect and Confront Error

If we know where we stand spiritually, no one can lead us off course. If we've gained enough spiritual knowledge, we can easily discern whether an idea, concept, or theory is true or false.

Knowledge Makes Us Confident in Our Daily Walk

For Christians, biblical knowledge builds spiritual confidence. If a person is stumbling along in the Christian life, constantly falling into sin and making mistakes, chances are they're not taking in the Scriptures; they're not well-grounded in the truth.

Knowledge Creates a Solid Foundation of Spiritual Truth that Filters Out Our Fears and Superstitions

Even in the twenty-first century, many people live their lives paralyzed by superstition and fear. Knowing God's Word helps us to decipher the messages we receive and determine whether or not they are of God. Scriptural truth rejuvenates us and keeps us from being drained of energy and immobilized by fear.

Which of these benefits do you think you need the most? Why?

[handwritten] — Love for people - less ups of...
— Confidence in my walk & my sanctification
Only if the Holy Spirit guides
— Boldness...

If your spiritual knowledge and wisdom were to increase dramatically, how do you think your walk with God would change? How would your relationships be different?

[handwritten] — Closer, less sin, more righteous Joy!
+ a peace!!!
— + Strength!
— My (His) love would guide out of them.

As believers, we're responsible to grow in our faith, knowledge, and maturity in Christ. The people we encounter every day desperately need to hear the message of God's grace and the hope that we have to offer. In fact, 2 Corinthians 2:15 goes so far as to say "we are a fragrance of Christ to God among those who are being saved and among those who are perishing." Learning Scripture is not just a luxury or a pastime; it's our delightful duty and our call as responsible, devoted followers of Jesus Christ. So let's plunge ahead with confidence, determined to learn more about God's Word and to faithfully share our newfound wisdom with others.

2

Don't Forget to Add a Cup
of Discernment

Selected Scriptures

If you've ever taken an art class, you know that one of the most difficult aspects of drawing or painting is trying to make a two-dimensional object appear three-dimensional. What's the difference between a two-dimensional object and a three-dimensional one? The first lacks a certain vital aspect: *depth*.

Our lives can become two-dimensional if we're not careful. They can grow devoid of depth and color and excitement. They can appear flat instead of possessing a well-defined purpose and shape. They can become unhealthy and imbalanced rather than vital and whole. This often happens if we acquire knowledge without the depth of discernment. To use a different metaphor, the recipe for a balanced, healthy approach to life requires that a cup of discernment be mixed in with our biblical knowledge.

Defining Knowledge and Discernment

Before we learn how to add discernment to our knowledge, let's define our terms. The Greek term *gnōsis* may be translated "knowing," "knowledge," or "understanding way." [1] For our purposes in this chapter, the word *knowledge* denotes the acquisition of biblical facts, principles, and doctrines. To gain spiritual knowledge, we must understand the themes and principles of Scripture so we can create a framework for accurately interpreting the whole story of the Bible. Knowledge is necessary, but knowledge does not take action or feel emotions. It results from acquiring and interpreting facts, and it will remain theoretical if we let it.

Now, let's explore the concept of *discernment*. We might describe discernment as a person's God-given ability to recognize and perceive the truth beyond what is said. Discerning people possess insight that reaches beyond the realm of the obvious. They can read between the lines. This type of discernment, rather than stemming from simple intuition, comes from the Holy Spirit. It flows from the wisdom He gives us—the wisdom of God. King Solomon asked Yahweh for this kind of discernment, as recorded in 1 Kings 3:9:

> So give your servant an understanding heart to judge Your
> people to discern between good and evil. For who is able to
> judge this great people of Yours?

Keep in mind that God had told Solomon that He would grant him *whatever he asked*. Did the king ask for money? Fame? Power? More possessions? A larger kingdom? No. Instead, he asked for the God-given ability to see situations with wisdom and spiritual discernment. Solomon recognized the importance of being able to judge people's hearts and motives, to see beneath the surface, to hear the hidden messages behind others' words. He knew that the gift of astute discernment would enable him to lead the nation well.

 If God told you today that He would grant your greatest desire, what would you ask for? How does your answer reflect your priorities and the attitudes of your heart?

_____

_____

_____

_____

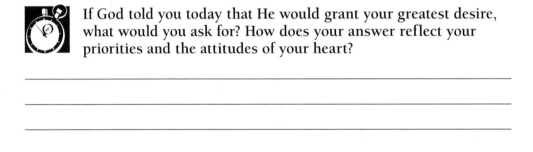

Getting to the Root

In Philippians 1:9, Paul wrote, "And this I pray, that your love may abound still more and more in real knowledge and all discernment." The Greek word that Paul uses here for *discernment*, *aisthēsis*, may also be translated as "perception." [2] When we practice biblical discernment, we harness the power of the Holy Spirit to perceive what would otherwise be hidden from view.

Those who possess discernment can size up situations, perceive problems, and spot evil lurking in the shadows. They can also sense truth and goodness. They can recognize excellent character. They can perceive personal maturity and depth—or the lack of it.

DISCERNMENT REQUIRES TESTING THE SPIRITS

Proverbs 2 mentions "discerning the fear of the Lord." First John 4:1 echoes this concept:

> Beloved, do not believe every spirit, but test the spirits to see whether they are from God, because many false prophets have gone out into the world.

Don't believe everything you hear. Put it to the test. Check it out. Think it through. Be wise. Just because a person is a pastor or teacher doesn't mean he or she is automatically a godly person. Just because a person writes with persuasion or speaks with charisma doesn't mean he or she lives a life of integrity. Don't assume anything; rather, "test the spirits" in order to determine whether or not a particular message is from God.

Unfortunately, there's no textbook formula for increasing your spiritual perception, but you can develop this type of awareness as you walk with God through life. One way to sharpen your discernment is to get spiritual input from more than one source. Refuse to blindly follow only one leader's teaching. If you drink at just one fountain, you will lose perspective. It's like eating only one food, or enjoying only one type of entertainment, or wearing only one color. How boring! Remember that Paul wrote, "I pray you'll grow in *real* knowledge and discernment." The Greek term translated as "real knowledge," *epignōsis*, means true, well-rounded, balanced knowledge.[3]

In your own words, describe some of the differences between knowledge and discernment.

_____

_____

_____

_____

We've all known knowledgeable people who made mistakes as a result of failing to exercise discernment. List an example of someone who was not spiritually discerning when making a decision. What were the circumstances? What was the end result?

_____

_____

_____

_____

What does it mean to "test the spirits"? Can you think of a time or a situation in which the Holy Spirit helped you to exercise godly discernment? If so, what was the outcome?

_____

_____

_____

_____

 ## In Case You Were Wondering

Q: How can I recognize false spiritual teaching and arm myself against it?

A: Scripture provides strong warnings against false teachers and lists some of their characteristics. Paul writes in Galatians, "There are some who are disturbing you and want to distort the gospel of Christ. . . . if we, or an angel from heaven, should preach to you a gospel contrary to what we have preached to you, he is to be accursed!" (1:7–8)

We often can recognize false teachers because they deny the Person or attributes of the Lord Jesus Christ. They may deny His authority. They may seek to diminish Jesus's nature by denying His humanity and/or deity. They may deny the existence of the Trinity. They may deny that Christ is the promised Messiah. They may deny His death, His physical resurrection, and His promised return. Frequently, they attempt to teach a more "palatable" Jesus rather than the *real* Jesus, and they say and do things that directly contradict God's Word. The apostle Paul tells us that Satan disguises himself as an "angel of light" by means of these false teachers (see 2 Corinthians 11:13–15).

Jude wrote: "For certain persons have crept in unnoticed, those who were long beforehand marked out for this condemnation, ungodly persons who turn the grace of our God into licentiousness and deny our only Master and Lord, Jesus Christ" (Jude 1:4–5). God calls us to be on the alert; false teachers exist and will continue to spread lies. While Christian leaders have a responsibility to guard the flock from false teachers, this does not absolve us of our personal responsibility to watch carefully for them. *There is only one way we will be able to spot false teachers: we must be knowledgeable concerning the truth of the Word of God.* We cannot become lazy and expect others to do our studying and thinking for us!

Digging Deeper
Finding Spiritual Balance

Let's take a few moments now to talk about *balance*. Spiritual balance involves remaining free of extremes and seeing the whole picture rather than focusing on only a part of it. Balanced Christians are realistic, gracious people. They listen when others talk. They express their concerns with prudence and patience. They give other people the dignity of holding a different opinion without putting those people down.

Balanced believers are serious-minded yet light-hearted. They know how to think wisely, but they don't let themselves miss out on life's joys. They realize that they don't have a corner on the truth. They also remain spiritually strong when testing comes.

Why is balance so important? Without it, we tend to veer toward misunderstanding or misinterpretation of the truth. Believe it or not, most heresy has its roots in truth. The truth gets off course when people take it to extremes, tamper with it, or "tweak" it to try to make it fit their personal preferences.

Which aspects of your life (spiritual, physical, mental, or emotional) do you feel may need to change in order for you to become a more balanced person? List some specific ideas you have for adjusting these areas.

_____

_____

_____

_____

SOME EXAMPLES FROM SCRIPTURE

Let's review what we've learned: knowledge plus discernment equals a balanced Christian perspective. Scripture provides us with positive and negative examples of balance. Let's start by examining two negative examples and then move toward the positive ones.

Negative Examples

3 John 1:9–11

The first negative example features Diotrephes, a leader who overstepped his bounds. The book of 3 John describes Diotrephes as a man who knew the truth but refused to submit himself to it. He loved to lord himself over others by wielding power and assuming an air of superiority. In doing so, he trampled over the other members of his church.

Diotrephes's abuse of power and lack of discernment brought grief to those in his church. In addition, his selfish acts brought rebuke and discipline upon him. In order to avoid falling into the same trap, we must guard ourselves against an attitude of inflated self-importance. Developing our discernment and humility will help keep us from committing the sin of pride.

In what ways was Diotrephes out of balance? What lessons can you glean from his mistakes?

_____

_____

_____

_____

1 Corinthians 1:10–17

The second negative example features the Corinthian church, a body of believers divided by petty arguments. This first-century church had all the knowledge and gifts required for the body to grow spiritually. Yet, as the apostle Paul lamented, it was still marked by division. Apparently, the church had divided itself into at least four factions, each of which had separate emphases, followed different leaders, and acted antagonistically toward the other groups. The individuals these groups followed were Paul, Apollos, Cephas (Peter), and Christ.

Paul condemned the Corinthians' discord, calling it "fleshly." He suggested that the people's emphasis only on knowledge had made them arrogant. In order to balance their knowledge, these Christians needed to add a strong dose of discernment coupled with loving concern for the welfare of others. We're called to do the same. Our words and actions should flow from the grace and love modeled by Christ.

In what ways were the Corinthian believers lacking balance? How can you avoid the same strife within your small group or church?

_____

_____

_____

_____

Positive Examples

Acts 18:23–28

The first positive example of a balanced Christian perspective features Apollos, a preacher with a teachable spirit. Apollos, an Alexandrian Jew, was well-versed in the Old Testament and the teaching of John the Baptist. Apparently, however, he knew little about Christ or the Holy Spirit.

Armed with imbalanced knowledge, Apollos preached fervently in the synagogue in Ephesus. When Aquila and Priscilla (a husband-and-wife missionary team trained by Paul) heard Apollos speak, they recognized some deficiencies in his understanding of the person and work of Christ and other aspects of the faith. So "they took him aside and explained to him the way of God more accurately" (Acts 18:26).

Apollos eagerly soaked up this teaching, and when he arrived in Achaia, he used his new theological understanding to "powerfully [refute] the Jews in public, demonstrating by the Scriptures that Jesus was the Christ" (18:28). His ability to discern the truth and apply it led to new evangelistic opportunities for Apollos. Like him, we must remain teachable if we're to be effective servants of Christ.

Which of Apollos's attributes would you like to model?

_____

_____

_____

_____

Acts 17:10–15

The second positive example portrays the members of the Berean synagogue, a perceptive body of Jews. After Paul and Silas left Thessalonica, they came to a city called Berea. Once there, "they went into the synagogue of the Jews" (17:10). The text indicates that the Berean Jews were much more open to the Christian message than were the Jews in Thessalonica: "Now these [the Berean Jews] were more noble-minded than those in Thessalonica, for they received [that is, welcomed] the word with great eagerness, examining the

Scriptures daily, to see whether these things were so" (17:11). When they heard the gospel from Paul and Silas, they tested it against God's Word and found it to be consistent. So they embraced it unreservedly.

Notice the pattern. The Berean Jews did not accept what they heard simply because some authoritative individuals had told them it was true. The Bereans listened intently to Paul and Silas, thought through their message, and compared it to the Scriptures. Once they were convinced that the Christian message was consistent with the other divine truth they knew, they chose to believe in Christ and were saved (Acts 17:12). Now, that's an act of discernment that definitely had eternal ramifications! We, too, should carefully consider what others say, examining their teachings in light of God's Word. In this way, we can achieve spiritual balance.

What spiritual lessons can you glean from the positive example of the Bereans?

_____

_____

_____

_____

THREE PRINCIPLES WORTH REMEMBERING

Let's summarize our study with some timeless principles that, when applied, can help guard us from becoming imbalanced in our acquisition of theological truth.

No One Person Has All the Truth

Excluding the omniscient God, no individual knows everything. This realization should lead us to drink with discernment from the doctrinal wells of various persons and ministries—a practice that can protect us from spiritual stagnation and illness of the soul. Spiritually healthy believers draw their knowledge and encouragement from a variety of trusted, biblically sound sources. There's wisdom and safety in taking counsel from several godly leaders.

No Single Church or Ministry Owns Exclusive Rights to Your Mind

Christ—rather than a church, parachurch ministry, or preacher—is your Lord and Master (see Ephesians 1:20–23; 5:23–24). This truth should make us wary of any person or organization that attempts to dominate or control our thoughts. Our allegiance is, first and foremost, to Christ. We can rest assured that any person or organization that tries to usurp our primary allegiance is not following God.

No Specific Interpretation Is Correct Just Because a Gifted Teacher Says So

The Berean Jews examined what Paul and Silas said without any apparent flak from these missionaries. The Jewish congregation's wise example should prompt us to check the claims and teachings of people today against the one standard of truth we have—the Bible.

How does your own life correspond with these three principles?

_____

_____

_____

_____

In what ways might you adjust your life in order to achieve the balance they promote?

_____

_____

_____

_____

The recipe of life requires a cup of discernment to balance our knowledge. With faith and love added to the mix, we'll soon be partaking of a delicious, healthy spiritual meal that provides nourishment to our souls. Not only that, we can share our recipe with others so they can experience the same satisfaction. Grab your measuring cup and get started!

SECTION TWO

THE BIBLE

3

GOD'S BOOK—GOD'S VOICE

Selected Scriptures

Who would you turn to if you were told you had cancer? How would you cope with the sudden death of a friend or family member? Where would you seek guidance if you unexpectedly lost your job? How would you find the courage to keep going if your mate handed you divorce papers? Where would you find strength, comfort, and guidance in times like these?

FOUR COMMON CRUTCHES

When we're blindsided by life's inevitable crises, we tend to use one of four crutches to help us manage our losses:

Escapism	We try to escape pain through denial, fantasy, substance abuse, or unhealthy behavior patterns rather than facing them head-on.
Cynicism	We become preoccupied with unmet expectations; left unchecked, our disappointment leads to a destructive tidal wave of resentment.
Humanism	We seek worldly, human logic to solve our problems; we may consult secular counselors and rely on the latest self-help books or similar aids in an effort to solve our problems in our own strength.
Occultism	We may turn to mediums, fortune-tellers, Ouija boards, tarot card readers, or astrologists for advice and insight; this crutch is extremely dangerous.

Why do you think people tend to lean on these worldly crutches when they face a trial rather than seeking God's wisdom?

_____

_____

_____

_____

Have you ever tried to depend on one or more of these crutches for guidance during a difficult time in your life? If so, which ones, and what were the circumstances?

_____

_____

_____

_____

Read Colossians 2:8–10. How might this warning apply to you now or how might it have applied to the situation you listed above?

_____

_____

_____

_____

In the long run, none of these crutches supplies all of the comfort, wisdom, and resources we need to help us handle life's demands. We have only one true source of comfort: God, through His true and timeless Word.

In Case You Were Wondering

Q: Why should I believe the Bible? How do I know that it's true?

A: We should believe the Bible because it's God's inspired Word, it claims to be true, and it proves itself to be true in the lives of believers. Paul wrote in 1 Thessalonians 2:13: "For this reason we also constantly thank God that when you received the word of God which you heard from us, you accepted it not as the word of men, but for what it really is, the word of God, which also performs its work in you who believe."

The prophet Isaiah calls God "the God of truth" in Isaiah 65:16. Our Father reveals His truth to us primarily through the Bible. In Matthew 4:4, Jesus attested to the truth and authority of Scripture when He said, "Man shall not live on bread alone, but on every word that proceeds out of the mouth of God." The psalmist also testified to the veracity of Scripture:

You are near, O Lord,
And all Your commandments are truth. (Psalm 119:151)

The sum of Your word is truth,
And every one of Your righteous ordinances is everlasting.
(Psalm 119:160)

God has no intention of hiding His perfect truth from the people He so lovingly created. He desires for every person on earth to come to a "knowledge of the truth" (1 Timothy 2:4), so He reveals His truth to us through His Word. The fact that He is Truth guarantees that He will reveal Himself as He really is, that His revelation will be perfectly reliable, and that what He says will correspond exactly to the way things are. At least four times in Scripture, we're assured that God does not lie (Numbers 23:19; 1 Samuel 15:29; Titus 1:2; and Hebrews 6:18). When the Almighty speaks, His words are true and accurate.

We can depend on the Bible as God's infallible, written guide for our lives. Let's take some time now to explore these truths theologically and practically.

WHAT MAKES GOD'S WORD SO DEPENDABLE?

What is it about the Bible that qualifies it as our foremost and final authority? The answer is found in the identity, inerrancy, and reliability of the Bible.

Its Identity

You may be surprised to learn that the word *Bible* does not appear in Scripture at all. The term means "book," and it refers to the collection of the sixty-six books that the people of God have historically accepted as the Word of God. What does the Bible call itself within Scripture? For an answer, let's look at several passages in the New Testament.

Luke 24:13–35

After Jesus rose from the dead, He came to two disciples who were traveling toward the village of Emmaus. As they walked together, Jesus, "beginning with Moses and with all the prophets, . . . explained to them the things concerning Himself in all the *Scriptures*" (Luke 24:27, emphasis added). A while later, the two disciples remarked to each other, "Were not our hearts burning within us while He was speaking to us on the road, while He was explaining the *Scriptures* to us?" (24:32, emphasis added). Jesus called the written record of Old Testament prophecies "the Scriptures."

 Getting to the Root

The term *Scriptures* in Luke 24:27 and 32 comes from the Greek word *graphē*, which means "a writing."[1] God did not allow His message to be passed down solely through oral tradition from generation to generation. He wanted Scripture also to be recorded and preserved in writing, and He made this happen by means of human agents as they were moved by the Spirit of God (see Exodus 31:18; 34:27–28; Isaiah 30:8–9; and Jeremiah 30:1–2; 36:4).

John 17:14–17

John's gospel reveals Jesus's longest recorded prayer. In it, Christ says to His heavenly Father:

> I have given them Your word; and the world has hated them. . . . Sanctify them in the truth; *Your word is truth.* (John 17:14, 17, emphasis added)

Jesus made a very bold statement here: God's Word doesn't just explain truth, it *is* truth (see Psalm 119:142, 151, 160). Of course, in our day, many consider truth to be relative; they believe that any given belief, teaching, or fact is true only for some people in some places and during some time periods. But the Bible purports to be true in an absolute sense. Its claims apply to *all* people, and its content is relevant for *all* times.

1 Thessalonians 2:13

In his first letter to the Thessalonian Christians, Paul penned these insightful words that help us understand the identity of Scripture:

> We also constantly thank God that when you received the word of God which you heard from us, you accepted it not as the word of men, but for what it really is, *the word of God,* which also performs its work in you who believe. (emphasis added)

Paul was saying, "The message I presented to you was God's message, God's very words!" We can be assured that this collection of writings called the Bible is God's Word — literally. When we hear it or read it, we're receiving *His* message, listening to *His* voice, and considering *His* thoughts. No other book on earth can legitimately make that claim. The Bible stands alone and above all other books in the world. We cannot find a more solid foundation to build our lives on than Scripture.

1 Peter 1:23–25

Peter's first epistle lends another characteristic of the Word of God:

> You have been born again not of seed which is perishable
> but imperishable, that is, through *the living and enduring word
> of God*. For,
>
> > All flesh is like grass,
> > And all its glory like the flower of grass.
> > The grass withers,
> > And the flower falls off,
> > But the *Word of the Lord endures forever*.
> > And this is the word which was preached to you.
> > (1 Peter 1:24–25, emphasis added)

The apostle Peter confirmed Scripture as *living* and *abiding*. It's everlasting! Nothing on earth will last forever except God's Word and human beings. Everything else, including our material possessions, will ultimately be destroyed. This fact should move us to place obedience to Scripture at the top of our priority list—above the pursuit of fame, fortune, power, prestige, and material things.

Which of the aspects of Scripture's identity listed below do you find most compelling? Why?

- **God chose to preserve His Word in written form.**

- **God's Word is truth.**

- **The Bible contains God's very words.**

- **The Bible is living and abiding.**

Its Inerrancy

We cannot gain a complete appreciation of the dependability of Scripture until we understand how God gave it to us. To get a handle on this, let's become acquainted with three key terms: *revelation, inspiration,* and *illumination.* Then we'll zero in on two biblical passages.

- The giving of divine truth to man is referred to as *revelation.* This is the *fact* of God's communication to us, which occurs through three channels: creation, Christ, and the Bible (see Romans 1:18–20; Hebrews 1:1–2; 2 Timothy 3:16).

- *Inspiration* occurred when the Holy Spirit moved human writers to write what God chose to communicate. These writers were the *means* God used to provide divine self-disclosure in written form, and that written self-disclosure (God's revelation) is limited to the Bible only.

- When we understand and apply God's truth correctly, we experience *illumination.* This is a crucial *purpose* of divine communication which still takes place today. However, because the sixty-six books of the Bible stand as the completed, written self-disclosure of God, the canon is closed and the creation of Scripture as we know it has ceased.

When we think about God using sinful man to accurately record His Word, we can readily see that the most critical issue regarding this process is *inspiration.* Let's focus on this doctrine by considering two texts. The first is 2 Timothy 3:16, which says in part, "All Scripture is inspired by God." We read in chapter one that the Greek word translated *inspired by God* literally means "God-breathed." All the writings that comprise the Bible were breathed out by God Himself.

Also, notice that the doctrine of inspiration applies to the words of Scripture, not to the human writers. People like Moses, David, Luke, and Paul were not simply inspired to write Scripture like a composer is inspired to write a song. Rather, God spoke through these men, utilizing their individual personalities and styles to produce exactly the words He wanted to say. How did the Lord do this? Peter tells us:

> No prophecy of Scripture is a matter of one's own interpreta-
> tion, for no prophecy was ever made by an act of human will,
> but men *moved by the Holy Spirit* spoke from God.
> (2 Peter 1:20–21, emphasis added)

The human writers of Scripture didn't just sit down and decide on their own to compose the books which make up the Bible. Rather, these men were *moved* by the Holy Spirit. The word *moved* in Greek is a nautical term often used in reference to ships at sea. It's used in Acts 27 regarding a shipwreck. When the ship had lost its sails and rudder and was at the mercy of the blowing winds and swelling seas, it still moved, but not of its own power. It was moved along, or powered, by an outside force. Similarly, the Holy Spirit gave the Scripture writers the impetus and the message to write, and He also supervised the process. The result? Divinely authoritative writings, without error in their original form. Put another way, Scripture records God's message infallibly through fallible human agents. We can have confidence that everything it says is absolutely true.

In your own words, describe the doctrine of inerrancy. How does the fact of the Bible's inerrancy add authority to your faith?

_____

_____

_____

_____

Its Reliability

Now that we've established the identity and inerrancy of the Word, let's explore its reliability. Where can we turn when faced with the trials mentioned at the beginning of this chapter? To Scripture. We can rest assured that Scripture is absolutely true and reliable in every matter it addresses.

God's Word is relevant to every issue we face today. Take a look again at Psalm 119. Notice the way it's structured. Each section is labeled by a letter of the Hebrew alphabet, from *aleph* (A) to *tav* (Z). If you were to read straight through this psalm, you'd encounter, in general, every one of life's major experiences. The writer wrestles with these trials but, at the end of each section, he testifies anew that he's relying on God's Word. In the Bible, God has lovingly spelled out precepts for us to live by; He's given us a way of handling grief, greed, loneliness, morality, unjust criticism, and so much more. We can depend on it. In fact, the Bible is the book by which all other claims—and all "crutches"—can and should be tested.

One Christian apologist summed up the situation this way:

> Every spirit or prophet who claims to give a new or different revelation is not of God.

> This does not mean that there is no truth in other religious writings or holy books. . . . The point is that the Bible and the Bible alone contains all doctrinal and ethical truth God has revealed to mankind. . . . All other alleged truth must be brought to the bar of Holy Scripture to be tested. The Bible and the Bible alone, all sixty-six books, has been confirmed by God through Christ to be his infallible Word.[2]

Now, that's a book in which we can trust completely and unreservedly.

Name a phase of your life during which the inerrancy or reliability of Scripture was tested. What were the circumstances? What was the end result?

_____

_____

_____

_____

Digging Deeper

The Benefits of Relying on the Bible

Returning to Psalm 119, we discover at least three benefits we can enjoy by submitting our lives to the authority of God's Word.

We gain stability.

Even when people oppose us and events take a turn for the worse, we can find strength in Scripture to stand firm (see Psalm 119:98, 110, 114–117). Are *you* relying on the Bible for authoritative, wise counsel and stability?

We gain insight.

If we commit ourselves to meditating consistently on God's Word, we'll gain greater insight and a deeper understanding of life (see 119:99). Are *you* studying the Bible regularly?

We gain maturity.

Our obedience to the Bible will result in maturity and wisdom reaching even beyond that of those who are much older than we are (see 119:100). Are *you* applying the timeless principles of Scripture to your life?

Name a situation in your life that you need to place into God's hands today. What lessons do you think He wants to teach you through this trial?

_____

_____

_____

_____

What changes can you make in your life in order to depend more on God and seek His wisdom through the Word?

_____

_____

_____

_____

As you learn to depend on God's Word and further explore the doctrines of the Christian faith, you'll gain greater stability, insight, and maturity to help you in your daily spiritual walk. Fleshly attitudes and ideas, worldly philosophies, and sinful activities will make way for godly attitudes, spiritual ideas, wisdom from above, and acts of grace that glorify God. Make a commitment today to stay attuned to His heart by reading and meditating on His Word. You won't regret it!

4

HANDLING THE SCRIPTURES ACCURATELY

Selected Scriptures

Many of us have experienced abuse at one time or another. The abuse may have been verbal, physical, sexual, emotional, or a combination of these. The hurtful words and actions that constitute abuse leave lasting scars on the abuser's victims.

One type of abuse has not received the critical attention it deserves. It's spiritual abuse, which occurs when people misuse and distort God's Word in order to control, wound, and manipulate others.

We've all known people who have twisted Scripture or taken it out of context, forcing a meaning onto a passage to try to make it say something other than what it actually says. We may have been hurt or manipulated by such attempts to control us using Scripture. Sometimes people distort Scripture without realizing it, but others do so with intentional malice and deception. In either case, the results are frequently the same: we or other people are left with the impression that the Bible teaches something it does not. And if we embrace the faulty interpretation or application, we run the risk of harming our own spiritual health and negatively influencing the faith of others as well.

Unfortunately, Scripture twisters can be incredibly difficult to spot. Instead of playing the part of a slick used-car salesman with a selfish agenda and ulterior motives, many Bible abusers are sincere, personable, popular, charismatic, and even theologically knowledgeable people. In fact, some of them may be your own friends, family, co-workers, or church members.

By learning how to handle God's Word accurately, we can avoid engaging in and falling victim to spiritual abuse as we become more mature in our walk with God. In this chapter, we'll explore some practical steps for becoming better students, interpreters, and appliers of the Scriptures.

Have you ever come in contact with Scripture twisters or Bible abusers? If so, describe the circumstances.

_____

_____

_____

_____

What made you realize that these people were not handling Scripture accurately and truthfully?

_____

_____

_____

_____

Did you grow in your discernment and understanding of God and His Word through this experience? If so, how? If not, why not?

_____

_____

_____

_____

CHALLENGING THE MISHANDLING OF SCRIPTURE

Bible abuse has been around for a long time. In Jesus's day, some of the most serious Scripture twisting came from the professional clergy—the Pharisees, the Sadducees, and the scribes. These men devoted themselves to the preservation and proclamation of Scripture. But in their attempts to interpret it, they often mishandled and abused it. On several occasions, Jesus confronted them on this issue, emphasizing their need to discover and apply the correct meaning of God's Word. Let's turn now to the gospel of Matthew and take a look at some of these confrontations.

Matthew 12:1–2

The Pharisees once spotted Jesus and His disciples picking and eating grain on the Sabbath. The Pharisees charged them with breaking the Law because, according to their rule book, picking grain on the Sabbath was not permitted except in the case of temple service or where life was at stake. Since neither exception applied in this instance, the Pharisees thought they had trapped Jesus and His followers. But Jesus refuted their charges with three references to God's Word that emphasized the heart behind the Law rather than the Pharisees' nitpicky, purely human interpretation of it (Matthew 12:3–8).

Matthew 15:1–2

Later, a group of Pharisees and scribes questioned Jesus concerning the disciples' failure to wash their hands before eating bread. The religious authorities viewed this omission as a violation of their traditional rules of conduct, but Jesus countered their attack by showing them that they were guilty of breaking *God's* law for the sake of keeping *man-made* laws (Matthew 15:3–6). After Jesus exposed and condemned the hypocrisy of these religious leaders, the disciples came and asked Him if He realized that He had made the Pharisees angry. Jesus's strong reply demonstrated that He had no tolerance for these hypocrites and their misuse of Scripture (15:7–14).

Matthew 16:5–12

Another passage in Matthew illustrates a different problem from those we have examined so far. In the previous passages, some of the *teachers* of God's Word were found guilty of twisting or misunderstanding its meaning. However, in Matthew 16:5–12, Christ spoke, and His *hearers* failed to grasp His meaning.

After Jesus had, on two occasions, fed thousands of people by miraculously multiplying a small amount of food into an abundant feast (see 14:13–21; 15:32–38), He warned His disciples: "Beware of the leaven of the Pharisees and the Sadducees" (16:6). The disciples thought Jesus was referring to literal bread, but He actually spoke of the Pharisees' and Sadducees' teaching (see 16:8–12). Jesus responded:

> How is it that you do not understand that I did not speak to you concerning bread? (16:11)

Because the disciples had not paid close attention to Jesus's words, they misunderstood Him. Similarly, we can misinterpret and misapply Scripture if we aren't careful. As we study Scripture, we should probe deeply for the meaning of each passage and use prayer and discernment, as well as Bible-study tools and other resources, to help us understand God's Word accurately.

 ## In Case You Were Wondering

Q: What should I do when I'm faced with "gray areas," or issues that aren't addressed in Scripture? How do I know if a person is abusing Scripture with regard to these issues by "teaching as doctrines the precepts of men"?

A: First of all, you can use a concordance, Scripture index, or Bible dictionary to help you look up specific topics or keywords to gain insight on a particular subject and find out whether or not the Bible addresses it. You must arm yourself with the truth in order to avoid being a victim of spiritual abuse. You can be certain that particular words, actions, and choices are wrong if they contradict what is taught by God the Father, Jesus the Son, the Holy Spirit, or Scripture. In addition, when a person chooses to become a Christian, God grants him or her the gift of spiritual discernment and sends the Holy Spirit to indwell that person. If the Holy Spirit convicts you regarding a particular action or choice and you don't feel complete spiritual peace about it, then most likely, that choice is not God's will for you. Don't ignore the still, small voice of the Spirit!

Bible abusers normally fall into two categories. Those with legalistic tendencies often *add their own rules and regulations* to Scripture, while people with liberal tendencies try to *minimize or detract from* what the Bible teaches. Both categories of deceivers will face strict judgment for their false teaching and misguided deeds. If the Spirit convicts you that a person's teaching may be false, or you feel uneasy when a pastor, teacher, or another person shares his or her beliefs about the Bible, don't ignore that sense of unrest. Examine Scripture and arm yourself with the truth of God's Word!

HANDLING SCRIPTURE ACCURATELY

Let's turn now to Nehemiah 8 in the Old Testament, where we find a prime example of a time when God's Word was interpreted accurately and respectfully.

> All the people gathered as one man at the square which was in front of the Water Gate, and they asked Ezra the scribe to bring the book of the law of Moses which the Lord had given to Israel. (Nehemiah 8:1)

Ezra did as the people asked, then stepped up to the wooden podium that the people had constructed for the purpose of reading the Law (see 8:4). From the events that transpired, we can make four relevant observations about how to accurately read and apply God's Word to our lives.

First, *accurately handling the Scriptures starts with reading them.* Standing behind the podium situated above the people, Ezra read from the Mosaic Law. The Hebrews "were attentive to the book of the law" (8:3), regarding it as God's holy message to them. Likewise, our spiritual lives can benefit when we read Scripture aloud, allowing God's Word to sink deeply into our lives. He speaks to us in new ways through His Word.

Second, *accurately handling the Scriptures includes having respect for them.* By constructing a podium for the reading of the Scripture and placing it at a level above where the people stood, the Jews indicated their submission to the authority of God and His Word. They also honored God by standing up "from early morning until midday" as the Scriptures were read to them (8:3–5). Then, they responded reverently to the reading of the Word:

> Then Ezra blessed the Lord the great God. And all the people answered, "Amen, Amen!" while lifting up their hands; then they bowed low and worshiped the Lord with their faces to the ground. (8:6)

The Jewish people did not worship Scripture, but they realized that they could not be faithful servants of God without submitting to the authority of His Word. It's the same with us! The level of our honor and love for the Lord will be indicated by the degree to which we respect, obey, and conform to His Word (see John 14:15; 1 John 2:3–6).

Third, *accurately handling the Scriptures means that the truth is explained so that all can understand.* As the Mosaic Law was read, interpreters "translat[ed] to give the sense so that they [the Israelites] understood the reading" (Nehemiah 8:8).

Getting to the Root

The Hebrew word for *translating, parash,* means "to make distinct, to declare, to make clear." [1] In Nehemiah 8:8, this term conveys the idea of taking something apart so as to make it clear and understandable. The Hebrew word rendered *sense* amplifies this definition, since it expresses the thought of shedding light on something which otherwise would be unclear.

The Jews needed Ezra and his interpreters to explain the Hebrew Scriptures to them because the people were fresh from seventy years of captivity in Babylon. There, the Israelites had learned to speak a foreign language, to think with a Babylonian mindset, and to live in a pagan, idol-worshiping culture. Therefore, certain linguistic, intellectual, and cultural barriers had to be broken down to allow the genuine communication of God's Word.

Today, we often confront similar barriers as we seek to understand and apply Scripture to our lives. But we can gain insight as we listen to godly preachers and teachers, read books, use study aids, and become involved in small groups and Bible studies that will help us build bridges of understanding from the Bible's original setting so we can apply it to our contemporary situation.

Fourth, *accurately handling the Scriptures results in obedience to the Scriptures.* The Israelites had been told by God not to grieve at the hearing of the Law but to celebrate the holiness of the occasion. So, following the reading and interpreting of the Law, the Hebrews "went away to eat, to drink, to send portions and to celebrate a great festival, because they understood the words which had been made known to them" (Nehemiah 8:12). They responded with obedience after hearing God's voice through His Word. Likewise, when we probe Scripture to seek understanding of what God loves and what He desires of us, we will obediently heed what we've learned.

Digging Deeper

Tools for the Trade

We can glean much from personal time spent in God's Word using the well-known Bible-study methods of observation, interpretation, correlation, and application. In addition, we can use certain study aids to help us properly interpret and apply Scripture to our lives. Serious students and teachers of the Scriptures can enhance their learning experience by using a Bible concordance, a Bible dictionary, an atlas, and some Bible commentaries to round out their study. The acquisition of these tools may involve some financial investment, but the cost pales in comparison to the benefits that accompany the clear understanding and application of Scripture. If you need help or more information on how to find and use these tools, ask your pastor or another trained ministry professional.

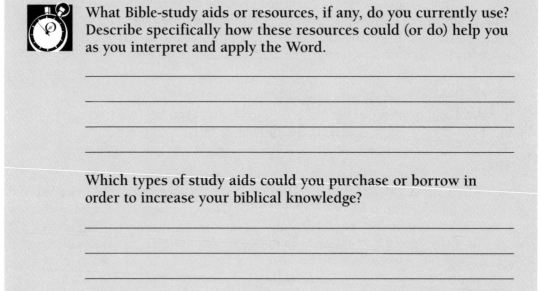

What Bible-study aids or resources, if any, do you currently use? Describe specifically how these resources could (or do) help you as you interpret and apply the Word.

_____

_____

_____

_____

Which types of study aids could you purchase or borrow in order to increase your biblical knowledge?

_____

_____

_____

_____

Make a list of the resources you need and order them the next time you go to a Christian bookstore or Web site. Insight for Living has many books, Bible-study workbooks, and other Scripture-based resources available for purchase at **www.insight.org**. You may also call our toll-free phone number, 1-800-772-8888, at any time to place an order for biblical resources. Our Web site also offers many practical articles and devotional materials related to living the Christian life.

Some Counsel to Bible Teachers

People who have been influenced by Bible abusers tend to become Bible abusers themselves. If you have been hurt in this way, refuse to channel your anger into harming others in a similar fashion. Seek to forgive those who led you astray, just as God has forgiven you of your own sins. Abandon harmful, abusive teaching and commit yourself to the lifelong pursuit of absorbing and applying the real truth and the magnificent grace taught in the Bible. You and those you come into contact with will be better for it.

How can we ensure that we'll be wise Bible teachers rather than Bible abusers? These five simple rules will assist you in your goal.

1. Never forget *what* you are handling.

The Bible is *God's* book. Recalling this fact will keep us sensitive.

2. Always remember *who* has the authority.

The divine Author of Scripture has the ultimate authority in our lives, and He has commanded us to obey His Word. This fact should make us humble.

3. If you are a Bible teacher, keep in mind *why* you are teaching.

Effective teachers don't teach the Bible in order to impress others with their knowledge or to cram their own opinions and theological ideas down their audience's throats. Rather, the goal of Bible instruction and study is to capture the original meaning of the text and to accurately interpret and explain it so that we can learn and apply its wisdom to our lives.

4. When you speak about God's Word, think about *where* people are.

People come from different families, cultures, backgrounds, locales, professions, religious pasts, and home situations. Keeping this in mind will help you communicate the message of Scripture in a powerful, relevant, and interesting way.

5. Focus on what happens *when* the teaching ends.

Once we have learned what the text says, we need to deal with its application in our lives. Only when Scripture is applied does it fulfill its whole purpose in the plan of God. And only then do we reap its full benefits.

Think back over your spiritual life. Regardless of whether or not you are a teacher, are you accurately handling the Word of Truth? If not, ask yourself what needs to change. None of us wants to be a Bible abuser. Instead, focus on being a conduit of God's love, grace, and truth as you study Scripture and share it with others.

SECTION THREE

GOD THE FATHER

5

KNOWING GOD: LIFE'S MAJOR PURSUIT

Selected Scriptures

Our society obsesses over self. Most of us do all we can to please ourselves, exalt ourselves, protect ourselves, and advance our own agendas. Our self-oriented pursuits illustrate that we're infected with a deadly disease: *me-ism*. Me-ism holds out the false promise of fame, fortune, and happiness. In truth, however, me-ism delivers feelings of emptiness and a greatly distorted picture of how life should be lived.

We'll never find out the real truth about ourselves until we start taking regular doses of the cure for the disease of me-ism: *the pursuit of the knowledge of God*. Do you want to know the truth about yourself, find lasting contentment, and accumulate treasures that can never be taken from you? Then take your eyes off yourself and fix them on the Lord. Until you do, your pursuits will be nothing but a frantic dash down a dead-end street.

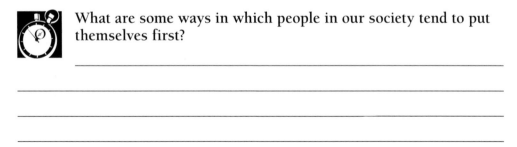 **What are some ways in which people in our society tend to put themselves first?**

_____

_____

_____

_____

Keep these examples in mind as we find out how the Israelites entered a downward spiral of me-ism that threatened to destroy them.

THE WAIL OF A WEEPING PROPHET

The prophet Jeremiah understood the value of making the knowledge of God his life's major pursuit. More than two thousand years ago, Jeremiah served the Lord in a nation gone awry. Although the Israelites knew God's Law, they had turned from Him to worship false gods and to pursue lives of sinful self-indulgence. Consequently, they brought divine judgment upon their land. Jeremiah wept over the Hebrews' spiritual obstinance and imminent demise, while at the same time wishing that he were miles away from his people and their wickedness (Jeremiah 8:13–9:3).

What was the foundational cause of the Israelites' spiritual disease? God made it absolutely clear: "They do not know Me" (9:3). Rather than seeking Yahweh and conforming their lives to His Word, the Hebrews chose to focus on themselves first. They adopted a counterfeit value system—one that exalted human wisdom, power, and resources over God's.

The Israelites' rehabilitation to spiritual health involved taking a simple prescription given by the Divine Physician:

> Thus says the Lord, "Let not a wise man boast of his wisdom,
> and let not the mighty man boast of his might, let not a rich
> man boast of his riches; but let him who boasts boast of this,
> *that he understands and knows Me*, that I am the Lord who
> exercises lovingkindness, justice and righteousness on earth;
> for I delight in these things," declares the Lord.
> (Jeremiah 9:23–24, emphasis added)

Getting to the Root

The Hebrew term from which *understand* is derived is *sakal*. It means "to be prudent." It also can mean "to act wisely; to discern; to prosper; to succeed."[1] The Hebrew word *yada*, translated "to know,"[2] refers to knowledge, perception, and insight gained through the senses rather than that gained solely through rational, intellectual thought.

When we link together the terms *understand* and *know*, we can see the cure for me-ism more clearly: all our faculties must be centered on and subjected to the living God. A person who truly *knows* God will understand and love Him intimately, just as a friend knows her best friend, a husband knows his wife, and a mother knows her child. Because God is the object of our knowledge and praise, we bow before Him in humble obedience and adoration.

In Case You Were Wondering

Q: Can you help me understand the doctrine of the Trinity? Where is this doctrine mentioned in the Bible?

A: Though the Bible does not actually use the word *Trinity*, it supports this doctrine in both the Old and the New Testaments. In A.D. 215, Tertullian (an early Christian theologian and writer) became the first person to use the actual term *trinity*. This term was created as a combination of the prefix *tri*, meaning "three," and the word *unity*.

In the unity of the Godhead, three coeternal and coequal persons exist (Father, Son, and Spirit) who are the same in substance but distinct in personality and roles. They are inseparable, interdependent, and eternally united in one Divine Being. This diagram shows an excellent early model created to illustrate the Trinity:

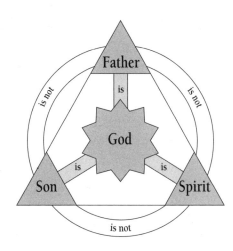

Many Bible passages attest to the existence of the Trinity. Moses and Job both use the title *Elohim*, which is plural, to refer to God. This title can be both a plural of majesty, emphasizing the Godhead's divine glory, as well as a reference to the plurality of persons within the Godhead. The plural Hebrew word *panim* (translated "faces," "persons," or "presence") is used to refer to God in passages such as Exodus 33:14–15 and Psalm 27:8–9. God says, "Let *Us* make man in Our image" in Genesis 1:26 (emphasis added), and the same usage occurs in Genesis 3:22; 11:7; and Isaiah 6:8. In Isaiah 48:16–17, the Lord God (*Adonai Yahweh*), the Holy Spirit, and the Redeemer (Jesus Christ) all are mentioned in the same context as distinct persons of the Godhead.

In the New Testament, John 14–16 contains repeated references to the Trinity, and perhaps the most compelling example in Scripture is the baptism of Jesus in Matthew 3:16–17, where the Father speaks from heaven and the Spirit descends in the form of a dove to rest on Jesus Christ, the Son, who is standing in the Jordan River after being baptized by John the Baptist. All of these biblical examples support the Trinity as a valid and vital doctrine, central to the Christian faith.

THE IMPORTANCE OF KNOWING GOD

Let's focus now on the blessings that are ours when we desire and pursue a more intimate understanding of our heavenly Father.

Knowing God Gives Us the Desire to Be Like Him

When the Lord refers to Himself in Scripture, He almost always specifies one or more of His character traits. When He does this, He frequently implies or even outright commands that we model ourselves after His moral attributes and example. Peter provides an excellent illustration of this principle:

> As obedient children, do not be conformed to the former lusts which were yours in your ignorance, but like the Holy One who called you, be holy yourselves also in all your behavior; because it is written, "You shall be holy, for I am holy." (1 Peter 1:14–16)

Knowing God Reveals the Truth about Ourselves

Isaiah 6 paints a vivid scene of God in all His glorious majesty "sitting on a throne, lofty and exalted, with the train of His robe filling the temple" (Isaiah 6:1–3). One of the seraphim, or heavenly beings, takes a burning coal from the holy altar, flies to Isaiah, and touches the glowing coal to the prophet's lips, saying:

> Behold, this has touched your lips; and your iniquity is taken away and your sin is forgiven. (6:7)

What an awe-inspiring experience! When we encounter God in all His glory like the prophet Isaiah did, we gain a better understanding of ourselves. When we draw near to His startling righteousness, purity, holiness, majesty, and brilliance, we suddenly perceive our own utter sinfulness and depravity. Once we have a more accurate appraisal of ourselves, our awe and knowledge of God will direct us to the One who has the power to meet our needs.

Knowing God Enables Us to Interpret Our World Properly

The Babylonian king Nebuchadnezzar learned the validity of this truth in a dramatic way (Daniel 4:28–37). Over the course of his rule, Nebuchadnezzar grew more and more self-centered and conceited. Rather than crediting God with his success, he praised himself. The Lord responded to Nebuchadnezzar's arrogance by causing him to go temporarily insane. The monarch became like a wild beast for seven years, even eating grass in the fields.

At the end of that time, however, God restored the king's ability to reason. Once Nebuchadnezzar realized what had happened to him and why, he praised the Lord, exalting God's everlasting sovereignty over creation. Likewise, when we come to know God for who He is, our perspective changes. We begin to see the world more as He does, and we start to realize that He's in control of all things—including us and our circumstances.

Knowing God Makes Us Stronger and More Secure

In the midst of Daniel's prophecy concerning Israel and her fight against foreign rule and religious oppression, we find this relevant truth: "The people who know their God will display strength and take action" (Daniel 11:32). David's psalms and Paul's epistles echo this sentiment. Those who depend on the God of Scripture find a source of power that enables them to withstand even the most vicious and unrelenting attacks on their faith.

Knowing God Introduces Us to the Eternal Dimension of Existence

Praying to His Father in heaven, Jesus said:

> This is eternal life, that they may know You, the only true God, and Jesus Christ whom You have sent. (John 17:3)

If we know who God is, we'll recognize His Son when we are introduced to Him. If we have believed all that the Father has said in His Word, we will believe in the Son and thereby become adopted children of God's everlasting family.

Digging Deeper

Longing for Heaven

Once we make the choice to establish a relationship with God by confessing our sin and believing in Christ's sacrificial death on the cross and His resurrection, we become heirs to God's eternal kingdom. This change of citizenship brings a perspective that begins to lift our minds above the temporal and renew them with the eternal. C. S. Lewis wrote:

> If you read history you will find that the Christians who did most for the present world were just those who thought most of the next. The Apostles themselves, who set on foot the conversion of the Roman Empire, the great men who built up the Middle Ages, the English Evangelicals who abolished the Slave Trade, all left their mark on Earth, precisely because their minds were occupied with Heaven. It is since Christians have largely ceased to think of the other world that they have become so ineffective in this. Aim at Heaven and you will get earth "thrown in": aim at earth and you will get neither.[3]

> **On any given day, how much time do you spend thinking about living in eternity with God? How often do you stop to consider the rewards you will receive for your earthly actions (see Colossians 3:23–24; Luke 6:35; Matthew 10:42)?**
>
> _____
>
> _____
>
> _____
>
> _____
>
> **How does Lewis's perspective help you shift your thinking regarding eternity and what's truly important in life?**
>
> _____
>
> _____
>
> _____
>
> _____

TACKLING THREE DIFFICULT SUBJECTS

In our humanity, we can't fully know God. After all, He's unlimited in every way, while we're limited in many ways. Aspects of His character, His acts, and His will remain mysterious to us as long as we remain on this earth.

Unfortunately, these enigmas, which are impossible for our finite minds to grasp, have prompted some people to abandon the truth and rationality of Christianity. God is eminently rational, and although orthodox evangelical Christianity does require faith, it does not teach anything that defies reason. Therefore, we're morally obligated to accept the enigmatic nature of certain aspects of faith without abandoning the rational aspects of Christianity.

Let's take time now to address three of the main Christian doctrines that can be somewhat difficult to explain.

The Glory of God

The "glory" of God indicates the presence of God. We see divine glory when God manifests Himself in creation and in history (2 Chronicles 7:1–3;

Psalm 19:1). God mysteriously reveals His personal presence in numerous ways: entering our world, initiating relationships with people, and answering our prayers. Yet He still exists apart from and outside of time and space.

The Sovereignty of God

Divine sovereignty concerns the plan of God. Our Father foreknows and maintains control of everything that goes on in the universe (see 1 Chronicles 29:11). Yet He does not force us to act in opposition to our will (see Genesis 3; Matthew 23:37; Acts 2:22–23). We shouldn't picture the almighty God as a cosmic puppeteer, manipulating us like marionettes on strings. Rather, He oversees creation without ignoring the free will and personal choices of human beings. The task of reconciling the mystery of God's sovereignty versus the free will of humans has baffled theologians for over two thousand years, and, in truth, we will never fully understand on this side of heaven how these two realities intertwine.

The Majesty of God

God's position is one of eternal and almighty majesty. He reigns above all beings and above all things. He is the authority over all authorities, the ruler over all rulers, the King of Kings, and the Lord of Lords (see Psalm 93:1–2; Ephesians 1:18–23; Colossians 1:15–18; Hebrews 8:1). Nothing can diminish or extinguish His greatness. However, we see glimpses of the Father's splendor only through His Son. The Son has revealed the Father and His love to man (John 1:18; 5:37; 6:45–46; 1 Timothy 1:17; 6:16).

SOME ESSENTIAL FACTS WE CAN APPLY

An accurate understanding of God should change our attitudes and behavior, not just our beliefs. With this in mind, let's examine some clear, practical truths that we can integrate into our lives.

First, *we please God when we walk by faith*. In fact, in order to please Him, we must have faith. And not only are we called to demonstrate that we believe *in* Him, but that we truly *believe* Him.

> Now faith is the assurance of things hoped for, the conviction
> of things not seen. For by it the men of old gained approval. . . .
> And without faith it is impossible to please Him, for he who
> comes to God must believe that He is and that He is a rewarder
> of those who seek Him. (Hebrews 11:1, 2, 6)

Write your own one-sentence description of faith. In what ways is your faith vital to your relationship with God and your spiritual walk?

_____

_____

_____

_____

Second, *we glorify God when we worship Him in truth*. When we can't explain something or when life seems unfair or overwhelming, God is pleased when we trust Him to get us through it. When we worship in truth, we come to our Father acknowledging life the way it is—we admit the good and the bad, and we worship God anyway.

When Jesus talked with the woman at the well, He told her: "God is spirit, and those who worship Him must worship in spirit and in truth" (John 4:24). What do you think Jesus meant? (You may want to refer to John 3:5–6 and John 14:6.) How can you worship this way in your own life?

_____

_____

_____

_____

Third, *God becomes our Father when we believe in His Son—and not until then*. When we choose to place our faith in Jesus Christ as our Savior and Lord, God sends the Holy Spirit to indwell us. The Holy Spirit living and moving within us empowers us to model Christ's attitudes and His actions to others. Paul touches on this vital truth in the book of Romans:

> For all who are being led by the Spirit of God, these are sons of God. For you have not received a spirit of slavery leading to fear again, but you have received a spirit of adoption as sons by which we cry out "Abba! Father!" (Romans 8:14–15)

The next time you find yourself focusing on your own desires, remember that knowing and loving God should be your life's major pursuit. Find some ways today to clear away the debris of "me-ism" and make your way to the throne of God.

6

LOVING GOD: OUR ULTIMATE RESPONSE
Selected Scriptures

We've already learned that we must know God in order to experience a lasting sense of purpose and meaning in our lives. However, simply having an intellectual knowledge of God isn't enough; we must act on that knowledge by *loving* Him. And that involves trusting, obeying, and worshiping Him with our entire being. Let's explore what the Bible says about how we can deepen and strengthen our love for God.

A FOUNDATIONAL STATEMENT AND COMMAND: TO LOVE

Deuteronomy 6:4–9 contains Scripture's foundational passage for how we should love God. This passage opens with a prayer known as the *Shema*, one of the most important creeds of Judaism: "Hear, O Israel! The Lord is our God, the Lord is one!" (6:4).

Getting to the Root

The Hebrew word *Shema* literally means "hear." The term used for "one," *echad*, is the same word used in Genesis 2:24 to describe the "one flesh" relationship of a man and a woman in marriage.[1] *Echad* stresses unity while recognizing diversity within that oneness. The term affirms that Yahweh alone is God and that He exists as three persons with one divine nature.

Next, this passage conveys the following vital command from the Lord:

> You shall love the Lord your God with all your heart and with all your soul and with all your might. (Deuteronomy 6:5)

Jesus echoed these words in the New Testament when a lawyer from among the Pharisees asked Him to identify the greatest commandment.

> And He [Jesus] said to him, "You shall love the Lord your God with all your heart, and with all your soul, and with all your mind." This is the great and foremost commandment. (Matthew 22:37–38)

Why do you think Christ describes this commandment as the greatest? What is so significant about it?

_____

_____

_____

_____

Read Deuteronomy 6:6–9. In what ways can we demonstrate our love for God and our commitment to learn His Word and pass it on to our children?

_____

_____

_____

_____

How do you think your life would be different if you consistently loved God with all your heart, soul, and mind and lived out that love daily? List some specific examples.

_____

_____

_____

_____

Jesus calls us to love God the Father with all we are and in all we do. He asks us to make the ultimate commitment to the ultimate Being. Centuries earlier, as noted in the passage above, Moses had exhorted God's people to demonstrate their love for Yahweh by meditating on, teaching, and obeying His Word. The message is the same today. Our lives should be characterized by what God desires of us. We're also called to instruct our children, by our words and example, on how to live godly lives.

Loving God: David's Response to God's Presence

Our love for God isn't a one-way street. Not only has He loved us first (see 1 John 4:19), but He loves us infinitely more than we could ever love Him back. David, the king and psalmist, frequently expressed his love and thankfulness to God. Much of the hymnbook we know as the Psalms consists of David's poignant songs of love and praise to the Lord. Here, we'll take a closer look at six of these songs. The first three (Psalms 31, 37, and 46) remind us of how graciously the Lord has loved us, protected us, and provided for us. The latter three (Psalms 18, 32, and 40) give us an intimate picture of David's relationship with God—a model for us to follow.

Psalm 31

In the opening verses of this psalm, David voiced his assurance that God would provide him with strength, encouragement, guidance, and protection (Psalm 31:1–4). He believed that the Lord would deliver him from the terrors that threatened to destroy his life (31:9–13). Rather than becoming intimidated and depressed, David turned to the Lord:

> But as for me, I trust in You, O Lord,
> I say, "You are my God."
> My times are in Your hand;
> Deliver me from the hand of my enemies and from those who
> persecute me. (31:14–15)

The Lord's faithfulness to David even in the depths of the darkest valley illustrates that our Father will never leave us in the lurch. Our lives rest in His hands. We can lean on Him no matter what, trusting in Him to deliver us from our enemies and to see us through every painful and disheartening trial.

Psalm 37

This ancient hymn teaches us that when we place our faith in God, He'll protect us, defend us, vindicate us, and bless us. But to receive this security, we must follow the counsel of the psalmist:

> Rest in the Lord and wait patiently for Him;
> Do not fret because of him who prospers in his way,
> Because of the man who carries out wicked schemes.
> Cease from anger, and forsake wrath;
> Do not fret; it leads only to evildoing.
> For evildoers will be cut off,
> But those who wait for the Lord, they will inherit the land.
> (37:7–9)

Because we live in a world full of spiritual rebels, we'll come under attack as we place our faith in God and then rev that faith into action. When we're attacked, we're called to respond to our assailants with caring hearts rather than with vengeful anger. In the same way that God loves us, we're called to love others (see 1 John 4:11).

Psalm 46

We can already see some of the main themes of the Psalms surfacing: trust, deliverance, faith, protection, waiting for the Lord, and seeking God's revenge on our enemies. Psalm 46 (by an unknown author) contains one of the most powerful word pictures in the book, depicting God as our fortress in times of need:

> God is our refuge and strength,
> A very present help in trouble.
> Therefore we will not fear. (46:1–2)

When we trust in the Lord as our greatest source of protection and power, He shows Himself to be worthy of our faith. As He rescues us from danger and meets our needs time and time again, our fears diminish, and we grow to love Him and depend on Him more.

Psalm 18

The superscription of this psalm says that David wrote it "in the day that the Lord delivered him from the hand of all his enemies and from the hand of Saul." We aren't told where David was; perhaps he had hidden in a cave. But it was God who truly kept him safe, sparing the future king once again from death. Overflowing with gratitude to the Lord, David poured out his heart in lyrical form:

> I love You, O Lord, my strength.
> The Lord is my rock and my fortress and my deliverer;
> My God, my rock, in whom I take refuge;
> My shield and the horn of my salvation, my stronghold.
> I call upon the Lord, who is worthy to be praised,
> And I am saved from my enemies. . . .
> The Lord lives, and blessed be my rock;
> And exalted be the God of my salvation,
> The God who executes vengeance for me,
> And subdues peoples under me. . . .
> Therefore I will give thanks to You among the nations, O Lord,
> And I will sing praises to Your name. (18:1–3, 46–49)

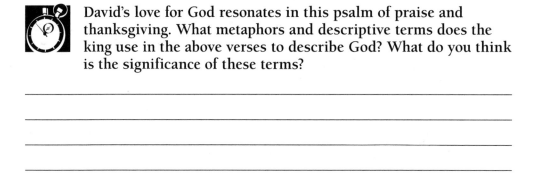 **David's love for God resonates in this psalm of praise and thanksgiving. What metaphors and descriptive terms does the king use in the above verses to describe God? What do you think is the significance of these terms?**

_____

_____

_____

_____

Psalm 32

This song was composed against a very different backdrop than Psalm 18. David had not been fleeing for his life, but lying to the Hebrew people. He had slept with another man's wife, Bathsheba, and had even gone so far as to have her husband, Uriah, killed so that he could take her as his bride. After the prophet Nathan finally exposed David's sin, the king readily confessed his wrongdoing and submitted himself to the Lord's discipline, forgiveness, and restoration. In response to God's gracious and merciful dealings with him, David penned these words:

> How blessed is he whose transgression is forgiven,
> Whose sin is covered! . . .
> When I kept silent about my sin, my body wasted away
> Through my groaning all day long. . . .
> I acknowledged my sin to You,
> And my iniquity I did not hide;
> I said, "I will confess my transgressions to the Lord";
> And *You forgave the guilt of my sin.*
> (Psalm 32:1–5, emphasis added)

The Lord dealt not only with David's sin, but also with the destructive burden of guilt the king felt as a result of his sin. Consequently, David no longer suffered under the staggering weight of this burden. Instead, he experienced the joy of divine cleansing and restoration.

Psalm 40

Although we are not told exactly what moved David to write this psalm, we do know that he composed it after the Lord delivered him from a long spiritual struggle (see Psalm 40:1–2). God, in His mercy, rescued David and strengthened him in his faith once again. Notice how David descriptively expressed his gratitude to the Lord:

> He brought me out of the pit of destruction, out of the
> miry clay,
> And He set my feet upon a rock making my footsteps firm.
> He put a new song in my mouth, a song of praise to our God;
> Many will see and fear,
> And will trust in the Lord.
> How blessed is the man who has made the Lord his trust.
> (40:2–4)

Describe a situation in which you felt similar feelings of joy and relief after the easing of a heavy physical, emotional, or spiritual burden. What were the circumstances? Did you express your thankfulness to the Lord for the deliverance He provided? If so, how?

_____

_____

_____

_____

 ## In Case You Were Wondering

Q: If God is sovereign, how can man have free will?

A: Scripture clearly asserts that God, our Father, is sovereign and has supreme rule over all of creation. The Bible says:

> The Lord has established His throne in the heavens,
> And His sovereignty rules over all. (Psalm 103:19)

> But our God is in the heavens;
> He does whatever He pleases. (Psalm 115:3)

> For I know that the Lord is great
> And that our Lord is above all gods.
> Whatever the Lord pleases, He does,
> In heaven and in earth, in the seas and in all deeps.
> (Psalm 135:5–6)

Sovereign means "possessed of supreme power; unlimited in extent; absolute; enjoying autonomy; independent."[2] God's sovereignty gives Him the power and freedom to do whatever He wants, anywhere, at any time, and to carry out His eternal purposes in every detail without interference. Out of His great love for us, He desires to establish a personal relationship with every man, woman, and child and to reconcile each of us to Himself through the person and work of Jesus Christ. He longs for us to follow Him and obey His Word, and yet He allows us the freedom to choose (or refuse) to live our lives in a way that pleases Him.

In his book *The Knowledge of the Holy*, A. W. Tozer used this illustration to explain how God's sovereignty and man's free will work together:

> An ocean liner leaves New York bound for Liverpool. Its destination has been determined by proper authorities. Nothing can change it. This is at least a faint picture of sovereignty.
>
> On board the liner are scores of passengers. These are not in chains, neither are their activities determined for them by decree. They are completely free to move about as they will. They eat, sleep, play, lounge about on the deck, read, talk, altogether as they please; but all the while the great liner is carrying them steadily onward toward a predetermined port.
>
> Both freedom and sovereignty are present here and they do not contradict each other. So it is, I believe, with man's freedom and the sovereignty of God. The mighty liner of God's sovereign design keeps its steady course over the sea of history. God moves undisturbed and unhindered toward the fulfillment of those eternal purposes which He purposed in Christ Jesus before the world began.[3]

The next time you doubt God's sovereignty or man's freedom of choice, remember that God has placed you on His ocean liner, but what you do on board is up to you!

THE MARKS OF A TRUE LOVER OF GOD

David's response to God's grace provides a worthy model for us to imitate. David shows us that those who have properly accepted and responded to the Father's love for them are those who really love the Lord. Reflecting on David's psalms, we can make at least three observations about those who have a genuine love for God.

- We who truly love God have experienced His power to deliver, so our fears are gone.

- We who truly love God have received His peace and forgiveness, so our guilt has been relieved.

- We who truly love God have felt His presence in the midst of trying times and, as a result, our faith has been strengthened.

Five Dimensions of Love

Essentially, the kind of love that God commands believers to express has five dimensions.

1. We're exhorted to love God with our entire being.

2. We're instructed to love our neighbors as ourselves.

3. We're called to love other believers.

4. We're encouraged to love our spouses and families.

5. We're commanded to love our enemies.

These five dimensions sound lofty, don't they? In fact, some of them seem downright unattainable at times. How can we love God with our entire being? How can we love other believers when they disappoint us? How can we love our families when they fail us? How can we love our enemies when they hurt us?

Choosing to love in these circumstances takes supernatural grace that can only come from God. We don't love God out of our own strength; we love Him because He first loved us. We don't love people because they're wonderful and they deserve it; we love them because God loves them and He has commanded us to love them, too. Others aren't perfect, and we aren't perfect either. But God calls us to have fellowship with one another within the community of faith and to reach out to those outside the community of faith. As we seek to incorporate all five dimensions of love into our lives, we reap the rewards of living a life of obedience and faith.

Digging Deeper

Loving God is Good for Your Health

Dr. Jeff Levin, an epidemiologist and former medical school professor, has found that a loving relationship with God may be an important key to enjoying better health. According to clinical studies, people who strongly affirm that they love God and feel loved by God score higher on a measure of overall health. The results, published in the journal *Review of Religious Research*, show that loving God can be a significant factor in a person's good health, even when other social, psychological, and medical factors are taken into account. Dr. Levin notes:

> There is a great potential for classical sources of human strength, such as love, to find their place into theories of health and healing. A loving relationship with God is held to be an especially potent source of well-being according to many of the world's faiths. This study shows, for the first time, that this is empirically true.[4]

Do Dr. Levin's findings surprise you? Why or why not?

_____

_____

_____

_____

Why do you think that loving God and feeling loved by Him can have such a positive effect on our health and sense of well-being? How do these emotions manifest themselves in our daily lives?

_____

_____

_____

_____

> **In contrast, what could we conclude about those people who have not experienced the love of God and do not have a relationship with Him? With this knowledge, how can you change the way you approach and respond to non-Christians?**
>
> _____
>
> _____
>
> _____
>
> _____

Every believer's life should be characterized by love. Love represents our greatest testimony to the lost and the most powerful contribution we can make to a confused, sinful, and dying world. We're called to have a passionate love for God, brotherly love for those in the faith, and compassionate love for those who do not know our Father. When we take the time to demonstrate true care and sacrificial love for others, we break down the barriers that once divided us and build bridges in their place.

Do other people know that you're a Christian by your love?

The Lord Jesus Christ

7

MARY'S LITTLE LAMB

Selected Scriptures

In 1809, the eyes of the world were riveted on Napoleon as the general pushed his way through Europe in a fierce pursuit of power. During the same year, William Gladstone was born, later to become one of England's finest statesmen. In the same year, Alfred Lord Tennyson took his first breath. His literary endeavors eventually left their mark on his world and the generations that followed. And a man who radically altered the course of history was born in a rugged log cabin that same year. His name? Abraham Lincoln.

As significant as these births were, none can compare to the birth of a baby boy that took place between 6 and 4 B.C. in the village of Bethlehem. At that time, the Roman Empire ruled most of the known world, clutching Europe, North Africa, and the Middle Eastern countries in its powerful fist. Hardly anyone cared about the tiny town of Bethlehem, much less the birth of a Jewish infant named Jesus—the one who would die on a cross for the sins of all humankind. As usual, however, God saw things differently. He inspired a physician named Luke to record in his gospel the facts about Jesus's birth and His purposes for coming to earth.

Who would you say are the greatest or most influential people alive today? What makes them and their contribution to society so significant? How have they influenced your life?

_____

_____

_____

_____

69

In what year were you born? Name some significant events that have happened during your lifetime. How have these events affected the lives of you and your family?

_____

_____

_____

_____

Keep these things in mind as we turn our attention to Luke's poignantly rendered story of the most significant birth in history and the powerful effect it had on all of humanity.

THE BACKDROP OF JESUS'S BIRTH

Luke links the birth of Jesus to a decree given by Caesar Augustus, the Roman emperor, ordering that a census be taken of all those who lived under Roman rule. Because the Roman Empire stretched from the Atlantic Ocean to the Euphrates, from the Danube to the Rhine to the Sahara Desert, this was a tremendous task. But, for taxation purposes, it was necessary that the Romans count and identify those people living under Roman rule. Censuses of this sort were taken periodically during biblical times, so Luke identifies this particular one as "the first census taken while Quirinius was governor of Syria" (Luke 2:2).

The Time of the Census

The census mentioned by Luke probably was taken sometime between 6 and 4 B.C. This date fits both Matthew's and Luke's chronologies, which indicate that the census and Christ's birth occurred shortly before the death of Herod the Great.

The Political Situation

The Roman Senate proclaimed Herod the Great as "king of the Jews" in late 40 B.C. However, Herod did not take control of Palestine until the summer of 37 B.C. when, with the help of the Roman army, Jerusalem was captured and Antigonus removed from power as ruler of the Jews. Always maintaining his loyalty to Rome, Herod reigned over the Jews for thirty-four years. Around

6 B.C., Caesar Augustus assigned Publius Quirinius the task of taking a census. The process of census-taking had always enraged the Jews because it combined the burden of Roman oppression with excessive taxation with the time, expense, and energy required to travel to each family's town of ancestry.

The Significance of Bethlehem

Centuries before Palestine became a Roman province, the Lord declared that a divinely appointed ruler would be born in Bethlehem:

> But as for you, Bethlehem Ephrathah,
> Too little to be among the clans of Judah,
> From you One will go forth for Me to be ruler in Israel.
> His goings forth are from long ago,
> From the days of eternity. (Micah 5:2)

Getting to the Root

We derive the name Bethlehem from the Hebrew words *bêt lehem*, meaning "house of bread." This village, located nine kilometers south of Jerusalem, was often called Bethlehem Judah or Bethlehem Ephrathah to distinguish it from other towns named Bethlehem, such as the one in Zebulun (see Joshua 19:15). The use of the term *Ephrathah* identifies Bethlehem as the town in which David was born (1 Samuel 17:12), thus establishing the necessary connection between Jesus, the Messianic King, and David.[1]

How incredible that the most significant person in all of history would be born in a little town like Bethlehem! But, because one of the census requirements was that all the people register in their hometowns and because Joseph was of the lineage of Jesse and his son King David, Joseph and his fiancée, Mary, made the eighty-mile trek to Bethlehem (see Luke 2:3–4).

In light of the events occurring in Palestine at the time, this couple's experience must have seemed trivial to most people. But Mary's pregnancy and Joseph's decision to take her with him to Bethlehem were part of God's plan to prepare the world for the birth of the Savior.

THE SCENE IN BETHLEHEM

When Mary and Joseph arrived in Bethlehem, they encountered a town bursting at the seams with people who had come to register for the census. The young couple looked for a place to stay, but all the usual lodging places were occupied. Desperate to find shelter for his expectant wife, Joseph finally discovered a stable—a cold, dark, smelly cave used to house animals. There, Mary gave birth to her firstborn son, wrapped Him in long strips of cloth, and placed Him in a manger—a rough-hewn feeding trough filled with hay.

Why do you think God chose a stable in Bethlehem for His Son's birth rather than a king's palace in Jerusalem? List several reasons why He may have done so.

_____

_____

_____

_____

Read Matthew 19:30; Luke 22:24–27; and 1 Corinthians 3:18–20. What messages do these passages convey about the differences between God's methods and ours?

_____

_____

_____

_____

How would you apply the truth of these passages specifically to Christ's purpose, birth, and work on earth?

_____

_____

_____

_____

MARY'S LAMB

As Joseph and Mary gazed in awe at their newborn baby, these weighty words from the prophet Isaiah must have flooded their minds:

> The Lord Himself will give you a sign: Behold, a virgin will
> be with child and bear a son, and she will call His name
> Immanuel. (Isaiah 7:14)

Immanuel — "God with us." *Jesus* — "Yahweh saves." Every time Mary or Joseph spoke these names or heard others say them, they would be reminded of the significance of their child in the plan of God. Here in a manger lay the Son of God in human flesh, born to a virgin. Mary and Joseph must have been overwhelmed with amazement as they sat and looked upon the peaceful face of their tiny, perfect child.

Nearby, some shepherds were "staying out in the fields and keeping watch over their flock by night" (Luke 2:8). Most likely, the shepherds were raising these sheep to be sacrificed at Passover, an offering ritual which foreshadowed the eventual sacrifice of the Lamb of God on the cross. Suddenly, an angel of the Lord stood before them, radiating the aura of God's glory. This awesome sight terrified the shepherds, but the angel said,

> Do not be afraid; for behold, I bring you good news of great joy
> which will be for all the people; for today in the city of David
> there has been born for you a Savior, who is Christ the Lord.
> (Luke 2:10–11)

The shepherds hurried off to find Mary and Joseph and the baby Jesus. Once they had seen Christ, they praised God and spread the word far and wide about the newborn Messiah. Scripture also tells us in Luke 2:19 that Mary "treasured up all these things, pondering them in her heart," foreshadowing the ministry of Christ that would eventually lead Him to the cross.

In Case You Were Wondering

Q: Is Jesus the only way to God? If so, how do we know?

A: Many passages of Scripture confirm that God has made salvation available to us by faith alone — faith in the birth, death, and resurrection of His Son, Jesus Christ, and the eternal, abundant life that He offers us. Probably the best-known passage supporting this truth is John 14:6, where Jesus says to Thomas, "I am the way, and the truth, and the life; no one comes to the Father but through Me." Other supporting passages are:

> God has given us eternal life, and this life is in His Son. He who has the Son has the life; he who does not have the Son of God does not have the life. (1 John 5:11–12)

> He [Jesus] is the stone which was rejected by you, the builders, but which became the chief corner stone. And there is salvation in no one else; for there is no other name under heaven that has been given among men by which we must be saved. (Acts 4:11–12)

> If you confess with your mouth Jesus as Lord, and believe in your heart that God raised Him from the dead, you will be saved; for with the heart a person believes, resulting in righteousness, and with the mouth he confesses, resulting in salvation. (Romans 10:9–10)

Christ came to earth, died, and rose again to offer us salvation. We believe God's Word to be true, and we experience the truth of Scripture's words, its claims, and its principles in our daily lives. Scripture claims that Christ is the only way to salvation; God claims that Christ is the only way; Jesus Himself claims in no uncertain terms that He is the only way; and the apostles and saints have affirmed throughout history that Jesus is the only way. If these claims are true, then the contradictory claims of other religions and philosophies that *they* are the only way (or alternative ways) to reach the same goal must be false. Jesus Himself taught that "the gate is small and the way is narrow that leads to life, and there are few who find it" (Matthew 7:14).

Christ is the only doorway to salvation, but the door's wide open! God wants every person to come to Him in faith, claiming redemption through Christ. The apostle Peter wrote in 2 Peter 3:9, "The Lord is not slow about His promise, as some count slowness, but is patient toward you, not wishing for any to perish but for all to come to repentance." Once we have chosen to walk through the door of salvation, we have the privilege of graciously sharing our message with others who may not realize or understand that Christ is the *only* way to God.

JESUS, THE LAMB OF GOD

We find the title "Lamb of God" just twice in the New Testament. Both occurrences appear in the gospel of John:

> The next day he [John the Baptist] saw Jesus coming to him and said, "Behold, the Lamb of God who takes away the sin of the world! This is He on behalf of whom I said, 'After me comes a Man who has a higher rank than I, for He existed before me.' I did not recognize Him, but so that He might be manifested to Israel, I came baptizing in water." (1:29–31)

> Again the next day John was standing with two of his disciples, and he looked at Jesus as He walked, and said, "Behold, the Lamb of God!" The two disciples heard him speak, and they followed Jesus. (1:35–37)

In each of these verses, John uses the Greek word *amnos,* or *lamb,* to refer to Jesus as the Lamb of God. The word *amnos* appears only two other times in the New Testament (see Acts 8:32 and 1 Peter 1:19). We can better understand the significance of this important title by placing it against the following background:

- *The Paschal (Passover) lamb of the Old Testament.* In Exodus 12, as the Israelites sojourned in the land of Egypt, God ordered each household to sacrifice an unblemished lamb and to smear the blood on the doorposts and lintel of their home. God promised that He would recognize the Israelites' obedience and the significance of the covenant represented in the lambs' blood by passing over those homes, protecting them from the slaughter of the Egyptians' firstborn children. The Lord swept through that night and struck down the firstborn of every Egyptian household. This horrible plague finally prompted Pharaoh to allow the Israelites to flee from the land of Egypt.

- *The Old Testament practice of offering a lamb as a sin offering.* (John 1:29 and 1 Peter 1:19 also make this connection.) Just as a person atoned for his or her sins by slaying and offering to God an unblemished lamb (see Leviticus 4:32), so we as Christians were redeemed from the death curse of our sin when we believed the truth that Christ, the unblemished Lamb of God, shed His blood for us on the cross.

- *The suffering servant of Isaiah 53, who was led like a lamb to the slaughter.* He refused to speak in His own defense and gave His life as an offering for sin (see Isaiah 53:7). Acts 8:32 contains a New Testament reference to this passage from Isaiah.

- *The image of Christ as the Lamb of God that appears prominently in the book of Revelation.* Here, we find this image or title used 28 times. In Revelation, a different Greek word (*arnion*) is used for Lamb, so the apocalyptic picture of a ruling and victorious lamb probably should not be read into the title "Lamb of God" in the book of John. Still, the book of Revelation clearly identifies this victorious Lamb as the sacrificial offering for our sin, stating: "You were slain, and purchased for God with Your blood men from every tribe and tongue and people and nation" (Revelation 5:9).

List some of the attributes of a lamb. What was the significance of using this title to refer to Christ? What does it tell us about His nature and character?

_____

_____

_____

_____

Digging Deeper

Recognizing the Significance of the Insignificant

If you take a look around, you'll discover that things today are much the same as they were in the days of Mary and Joseph. Few people seem to know or care about God's purposes, plan, or work in the world. Even at Christmas, the traditional celebration of Christ's birth, one hardly hears mention of Jesus or the reason He came to earth. People scour the stores for towering Christmas trees, lighted Santas, sleighs pulled by Rudolph and his furry friends, and snowmen dressed in hats and scarves. Yet the tiny figure of Christ in the manger is tossed aside. The smallest and humblest—yet most vital—element of the nativity scene fails to capture our attention or receive our worship for more than a few moments.

What about you? What place does Christ have in the overall scheme of your life? Truthfully, all of us prioritize worldly things over Christ at some time or another in our lives. What specific idol tends to lure you? Do you spend most of your time pursuing the material, the insignificant, the temporal, and the perishable? Do you tend to get caught up in material goods and glittery trappings and push Jesus aside? Are you letting the urgent things of life crowd out what should be your greatest and most important pursuit—Christ, the glorious Lamb of God?

Spend a few minutes reflecting on these questions. Write your thoughts below.

_____

_____

_____

_____

If you haven't yet made God the center of your life, you need to know that nothing is more freeing and life-changing. If you have never trusted Christ as your Savior, consider doing so now. Turn to the "How to Begin a Relationship with God" section at the end of this workbook. If you have already made Mary's Lamb your personal Savior, take a few minutes to reflect on Christ's sacrifice for you on the cross. Quiet your heart and your spirit before God and seek to focus on Him first, above the din of your everyday life. Put Him first daily by submitting your life to Him and the truth of His Word.

Mary's little Lamb wasn't just another Jewish baby born in Bethlehem. He lived, died, and rose from the dead in order to save us from our sins and offer us new life. In all of human history, no other person has influenced or radically, eternally changed as many lives. Has He changed yours? If so, does it show?

8

WHEN THE GOD-MAN WALKED AMONG US

Selected Scriptures

Most of the world's major religions follow a great, but fallible human leader. Every single one of these leaders, while they may have led lives of spiritual distinction, died just like any other man or woman has done. None of them have conquered death — none of them, that is, except Jesus Christ.

In contrast with all of the world's religions, Christianity depends absolutely on the person and work of the perfect God-Man, Jesus Christ, who died for our sins and rose from the dead to offer us salvation as a free gift. Author and theologian John R. W. Stott explains:

> Essentially Christianity is Christ. The person and work of Christ
> are the rock upon which the Christian religion is built. If he is
> not who he said he was, and if he did not do what he said he
> had come to do, the foundation is undermined and the whole
> superstructure will collapse. Take Christ from Christianity, and
> you disembowel it; there is practically nothing left. Christ is
> the centre of Christianity; all else is circumference.[1]

WHO IS JESUS CHRIST?

Who is this One who is so singular, so special, so indispensable? Let's turn to the Bible and find out.

Who Others Said He Was

The pages of history teem with various answers to this question. From the day of His birth, Jesus has been identified and labeled in many ways: a good teacher; a miracle worker; a misguided prophet; a carpenter from Nazareth; a man empowered by evil spirits; Christ, the Son of God; and the list goes on. The gospels record many of these characterizations, as well as Christ's claims regarding His own identity. Let's look more closely at the gospel records to gain more insight into who history said Jesus really was.

Who	Passage	Who They Said He Was	Response
The Wise Men (Magi)[2]	Matthew 2:1–12	The long-awaited "King of the Jews" (Matthew 2:2)	Seeing His star in the east, they traveled to worship Him.
The Pharisees	Matthew 9:34; 12:23–24	Called Him "teacher" or "rabbi" but also accused Him of demon possession. (See Jesus's response in Matthew 12:25–26.)	Skepticism, condemnation
John the Baptizer	John 1:29, 34 Matthew 11:2–6	"The Lamb of God who takes away the sin of the world," "the Son of God"	Proclaimed Jesus's deity as the promised King who would bless and judge; later he asked Jesus to confirm His identity (Matthew 11:2–6).
Neighbors, immediate family	Matthew 13:54–56 Mark 3:21	A "carpenter's son" who had "lost His senses"	Skeptical that this man they had known for years suddenly claimed He was God, they tried to remove Him from the public eye.
Herod Antipas the Tetrarch	Matthew 14:1–2	Feared Jesus was John the Baptist who had come back from the dead to exact judgment and revenge for his execution.	Fear, disbelief
The general public	Matthew 16:13–14	According to the disciples' report, "some [said] John the Baptist; and others, Elijah; but still others, Jeremiah or one of the prophets." But few grasped that He was God.	Curiosity, skepticism, some belief
Peter the Disciple	Matthew 16:16	"You are the Christ, the Son of the living God."	Devotion, belief, followed Him

Who	Passage	Who They Said He Was	Response
Citizens of Jerusalem at time of Jesus's triumphal entry into the city	Matthew 21:1–11	Some recognized Jesus as the Messiah; many were unsure. Most who waved palm branches did so because they believed that, if He truly were the Messiah, He would usher in an earthly kingdom that would overthrow the oppressive rule of the Romans.	Once the people found out that political victory was not Christ's intention, they quickly turned against Him.
Caiaphas the High Priest (head of the Sanhedrin, the ruling religious body)	Matthew 26:63–68	Interrogated Jesus about his identity. Jesus acknowledged that He was the Messiah who would reign with God and return as the judge of mankind.	In a fit of rage, Caiaphas tore his robes and charged Christ with blasphemy. Then they beat Jesus and dedicated themselves to having Him put to death.
Pilate	Matthew 27:11–26, 37 John 18:28–19:22	Concluded that Jesus had done nothing to warrant civil punishment, saying, "Why, what evil has He done?" (Matthew 27:23).	After declaring himself innocent of Jesus's blood, Pilate ordered Jesus's crucifixion. A sign was nailed to the cross, saying: "Jesus, the King of the Jews." The chief priests tried to get Pilate to change the wording of the sign, but he would not (John 19:19–22).

Who God Said He Was

When Jesus was about thirty years of age, He went to the Jordan River to be baptized by John the Baptist (Matthew 3:13; Luke 3:21–22). As Christ came out of the water, a voice from heaven said, "This is My beloved Son, in whom I am well-pleased" (Matthew 3:17). God the Father, the One who cannot lie, acknowledged that Jesus was His Son and was of the same divine essence as Himself.

Jesus Himself testified over and over again that He was indeed God in the flesh. During His ministry, He consistently revealed His true nature and, after His resurrection, He explained it more fully. Three days after Jesus's death and burial, Mary Magdalene and several other women found His tomb empty, and two angels informed them that Christ had risen from the dead. Soon afterward, Christ demonstrated to the eleven disciples that He had physically risen from the grave (Luke 24:36–43; compare to Acts 1:1–3). Then He turned their focus toward the Old Testament, helping them to realize that He was the Messiah spoken about in the Scriptures (Luke 24:44–47). He verified His identity by fulfilling prophecy, living a sinless life, teaching with supernatural authority, forgiving sins, healing diseases, raising the dead and performing other miracles, dying on the cross for our sins, and rising from the dead to conquer sin and offer us the gift of eternal life.

Getting to the Root

The name *Jesus Christ* is a combination of the name *Jesus* ("of Nazareth") and the title *Christ* in Greek, which means "anointed."[3] By calling Jesus "the Christ," as recorded in Matthew 16:16, Peter illustrated that he understood, at least in some measure, Christ's deity and the messianic significance of His work on earth.

Examples of Christ's Humanity and Deity

The gospels contain many illustrations of the fact that Jesus was both fully God and fully man. Let's probe further into some examples from each gospel.

Matthew

In Matthew 14:22–33, we see Jesus climbing up a mountainside alone to pray. The fact that He brings petitions before God the Father demonstrates not only His obedience and His desire to set a positive example for the disciples and for us, but it also illustrates His humanness. Mankind cannot even breathe on its own without God's sustaining power (compare John 15:5; Colossians 1:17). We can see from Scripture that Christ was fully man, yet He was also fully God.

Meanwhile, as Jesus prayed on the mountainside, His disciples found themselves trapped in a severe storm while sailing across the lake. Christ responded by walking toward them across the water and even causing Peter to walk on the water with Him! After joining the disciples in the boat, Jesus stopped the storm and calmed their anxious hearts. Christ's exercise of authority over nature immediately prompted the disciples to worship Him and acknowledge His deity.

Mark

In Mark 1:40–42, a man approached Jesus, begging to be cleansed of leprosy. The man's choice of words, "Make me clean," illustrates the deeper spiritual issues at stake. In the Old Testament, leprosy was sometimes used as an illustration of sin. Anyone who had the dreaded disease was to be ostracized from the Jewish community, according to Leviticus 13:45–46. This man violated the Mosaic Law by approaching Christ, beseeching the Savior to heal him. Looking down on the leper kneeling before Him, Jesus saw past the disfigured stumps where toes or fingers once were. He looked into the desperate, tear-stained face and saw a child of the King, one with a heart filled with faith and a body in dire need of restoration. So Jesus reached out with compassion and healed the leper.

Luke

In Luke 8:22–25, Jesus got into a boat with His disciples and told them to sail to the other side of the lake. Christ fell asleep during their trip, His exhaustion revealing His humanity once again (compare Psalm 121:2–4). The ripples splashing against the side of the boat soon became life-endangering waves that threatened to flood the vessel. The disciples panicked and woke their Master in fear. Jesus authoritatively commanded the storm to stop, and it did. Calm returned to the lake while the disciples, overcome with terror and awe, asked one another, "Who then is this, that He commands even the winds and the water, and they obey Him?" The disciples were right to ask this question, because they had just seen a man do something they knew only God could do. Jesus's act emphasized His deity.

John

In John 11:3, Jesus received word that Lazarus, His close friend, was sick. Surprisingly, the Lord delayed going to him for two days, lingering long enough for Lazarus to die. Arriving at the outskirts of Bethany, Jesus encountered Lazarus's sisters, Martha and Mary, both of whom seemed to blame Him for allowing their brother to die. The sight of the grief-stricken women and the Jews in mourning stirred Christ's deepest emotions, and He wept openly. This again revealed His humanity.

Then, Jesus made a surprising move; He commanded the mourners to remove the stone covering the entrance to the tomb. He paused, raised His eyes heavenward, and thanked His Father for hearing His prayer. Then, with the authority of deity, He shouted "Lazarus, come forth!" and the impossible happened. The friend who had been dead for four days appeared at the mouth of the tomb, wrapped in funeral garb, but alive! The Son of God had spoken.

Why do you think Jesus delayed in going to see Lazarus, Martha, and Mary? In what ways was His plan (God's plan) greater than their human plan?

_____

_____

_____

_____

Digging Deeper

Examining the Verdict of History

No individual in human history has encountered more controversy concerning His identity than Jesus. Though many have believed Him to be who He said He was—the Son of God—others have viewed Him as nothing more than a godly man, a wise moral teacher, or even a magician of sorts. C. S. Lewis has pointed out the fallacy with this kind of thinking:

> People often say about Him: "I'm ready to accept Jesus as a great moral teacher, but I don't accept His claim to be God." That is the one thing we must not say. A man who was merely a man and said the sort of things Jesus said would not be a great moral teacher. He would either be a lunatic—on a level with the man who says he is a poached egg—or else he would be the Devil of Hell. You must make your choice. Either this man was, and is, the Son of God: or else a madman or something worse. You can shut Him up for a fool, you can spit at Him and kill Him as a demon; or you can fall at His feet and call Him Lord and God. But let us not come with any patronising nonsense about His being a great human teacher. He has not left that open to us. He did not intend to.[4]

What definitions of Christ's identity or explanations of His ministry and miracles have you heard besides the traditional Christian view?

_____

_____

_____

_____

Why do you think people try to explain away Jesus's deity instead of embracing it?

_____

_____

_____

_____

If you're not living according to the knowledge that Jesus truly is God rather than just a great moral teacher or miracle worker, what changes could you make in order to better glorify Him?

_____

_____

_____

_____

In Case You Were Wondering

Q: I understand that Jesus Christ is much more than just a "great moral teacher," but how do I know that He's the true Messiah prophesied about in Scripture?

A: We can look back at Old Testament prophecies and discern two distinct lines of prophecy regarding the coming of the Messiah. One line predicted the first coming of the Messiah as the suffering Savior who would redeem His people by dying on the cross and then rising from the dead (see Psalm 22; Isaiah 52:13–53:12). The other line of prophecy foretold the eternal kingdom that the Messiah would establish after He had atoned for the sins of His people (see Isaiah 9:6–7; Daniel 7:13–14).

These two lines of prophecy concerning the Messiah were not fully understood by the Old Testament saints, but we understand them now because of the testimonies of the gospel writers and the explanation of prophecies by the apostle Paul. When the Lord Jesus Christ presented Himself to the nation Israel, He did so as their promised Messiah. In Luke chapter 4, He presented Himself as the fulfillment of Isaiah's prophecy (also see Isaiah 61:1–2). By His works, Jesus validated His power and authority to make such a claim. By His teaching, He revealed the true nature of His Messiahship and His eternal kingdom.

However, most Israelites had a different kind of Messiah in mind. They sought a Messiah of earthly magnificence, unlimited power, and military might, rather than one of humility who emptied Himself of glory to come to earth, take on human flesh, and die to save us from our sins (see Philippians 2:5–8). Consequently, some people began to withdraw from Christ, and the Jewish leadership in His day quickly began to resist Him as a threat to their concept of who the Messiah "should be."

None of this caught Christ by surprise. He knew that He must first suffer before He could reign. Jesus began to withdraw from ministry to the masses and to pour His life into His disciples. He began to teach the crowds in the mysterious, veiled language of parables. He spoke less about His earthly kingdom and more about His plan for the church. He dealt less with Jews and more with Gentiles. He rebuked the Jewish leaders more openly, revealing their error. He even willingly submitted to the Father's plan and accepted death at the hands of His opponents—just as the Scriptures predicted the Messiah would do.

The Bible records and supports the authentication of Jesus Christ as Israel's Messiah, as well as His presentation of Himself as the Son of God and His rejection by His own people. All of these events fulfill the Old Testament prophecies concerning the Messiah and confirm that Jesus truly was the long-awaited One referred to in the Old Testament Scriptures.

In your own words, who would you say Jesus is?

_____

_____

_____

_____

How do you apply this understanding of Christ's attributes, identity, and purposes to your everyday life?

_____

_____

_____

_____

History and Scripture have declared a clear verdict: Christ is the God-Man, the Messiah, the Savior, our Lord, and the Redeemer of the world. Now, let's make a commitment to love Him and live like we believe He is who He says He is!

9

Changing Lives Is Jesus's Business

Selected Scriptures

Changing people's hearts and lives is the Lord's specialty. Because He wants us to grow in godliness, He takes an active role in helping us toward this goal. Sometimes the growth process produces pain. Sometimes, we struggle to see God's hand at work. So, how can we be sure He's still at work in us or that what He's doing is accomplishing a good result? Because changing hearts is His business. He loves us too much to let us stay as we are.

Let's briefly examine some biblical tests that reveal our Father's personal involvement in our lives and the ways in which He helps us grow, mature, and change to become more like Himself.

God Is Committed to Changing Lives

During Jeremiah's ministry, the Lord commanded this Old Testament prophet to visit a potter's house (Jeremiah 18:1–2). There, the prophet watched a potter skillfully mold a lump of clay into a pot. When a flaw appeared in the vessel, the potter pressed and prodded the clay, reshaping it until the clay formed a useful pot that pleased him (18:4). Then God said to His people through Jeremiah:

> Can I not, O house of Israel, deal with you as this potter does? . . . Behold, like the clay in the potter's hand, so are you in My hand, O House of Israel. (18:6)

As the object of God's care, the Hebrews belonged to the Lord. He promised to continue shaping them into the kind of people He desired them to be, even if that required the firm hand of divine discipline.

The prophet Isaiah also used the imagery of clay being shaped by a potter. He recognized God as the Creator and Molder of His people:

> But now, O Lord, You are our Father,
> We are the clay, and You our potter;
> And all of us are the work of Your hand. (Isaiah 64:8)

Getting to the Root

The Hebrew word for potter, *yatsar*, is derived from a primitive root meaning "to form or fashion." The word is translated in various biblical contexts as "Creator," "Maker," and "potter"—meaning one who forms or fashions a vessel.[1]

GOD CHANGES US FOR OUR GOOD

We like to think that we're in control of our lives and our circumstances, but Scripture reminds us otherwise. In Romans 8:28–30, the apostle Paul wrote:

> We know that God causes all things to work together for good to those who love God, to those who are called according to His purpose. For those whom He foreknew, He also predestined to become conformed to the image of His Son, so that He would be the firstborn among many brethren; and these whom He predestined, He also called; and these whom He called, He also justified; and these whom He justified, He also glorified.

Few biblical promises offer believers more assurance than these. Remember: God doesn't just cause *some* things to work for good. He tells us that *all* things will work out for good within His sovereign plan. And we find other relevant promises in these verses as well. God specifically has called us according to His purposes. He knew us and He had a plan for us before we were even conceived, and He continues to shape us and conform us to the image of His Son.

Digging Deeper
What's the Shape of Your Heart?

The great painter and sculptor Michelangelo described the creation of one of his masterpieces this way: "I saw the angel in the marble and carved until I set him free."[2] We can think of God as our divine sculptor, taking his chisel and tapping away at the marble of our lives until a lovely form takes shape.

When we look in the mirror, we may see a chunk of shapeless, useless stone, but God sees our potential. He knows that inside that block of rock, there's a stunning masterpiece just waiting to be discovered, and He chisels off our rough edges until He sets us free. God wants His people to have His character, and He will not stop working toward this objective until it is accomplished in the life of every believer.

In fact, God is so involved in the lives of Christians that he refers to us in Ephesians 2:10 as "His workmanship." He has made us His pet project. We've been created in Christ Jesus to do the good works that God has prepared for us to do.

In Philippians 1:6, the apostle Paul assures us that what God starts, He finishes. He will not walk away from us. He promises to pursue us, woo us, shape us, purge us of sin, refine us with fire, and polish us until he perfects us in the day of Christ Jesus.

Think about the images of God as a potter and a sculptor. What are the qualities He possesses that enable Him to shape us?

_____

_____

_____

_____

> **Now, think of yourself as the lump of clay or the block of marble from which God is creating a masterpiece. What qualities must you possess in order for you to be shaped easily by Him?**
>
> _____
>
> _____
>
> _____
>
> _____

THREE LIVES THAT JESUS CHANGED

Let's move now to some New Testament examples of lives that Jesus changed. In the gospel of John, we discover three people whose lives Jesus radically transformed by reaching out and offering His healing, reassuring, forgiving, and grace-filled touch. Although these individuals differed from one another in significant ways, the divine Potter expertly molded them in His hands.

A Wayward Woman

During the heat of the day, a Samaritan woman came to draw water from a local well (John 4:7). Jesus sat by the well, resting from His arduous journey. He asked the Samaritan woman for a drink.

This woman knew that, according to Jewish law, any Jew who drank from her water vessel would be considered ceremonially unclean (John 4:9). Jesus had grabbed her full attention. He continued:

> If you knew the gift of God, and who it is who says to you,
> "Give Me a drink," you would have asked Him, and He would
> have given you living water. (4:10)

Jesus offered this Samaritan woman life-giving water! Then, He proved His deity by revealing His intimate knowledge of her past (4:15–18). He was putting into action His work of changing lives. She said to Him, "Sir, I perceive that You are a prophet" (4:19). Jesus's words had raised Him to the status of a prophet in her eyes.

The Samaritan woman tried to sidetrack Jesus by raising an ancient religious issue that was still a matter of friction between the Jews and the Samaritans: the proper place of worship (John 4:20). The Samaritans believed that Abraham had offered Isaac as a sacrifice on Mount Gerizim in Samaria. But Genesis 22 states that the sacrifice was offered on Mount Moriah in Jerusalem. The Samaritans regarded Mount Gerizim as the most sacred place on earth, while the Jews regarded Jerusalem the same way. This disagreement caused so much friction between the two cultures that they despised each other.

Next, Jesus told her that the kind of worshipers God seeks are those who worship in spirit and truth. And, remarkably, He declared Himself as the Messiah (John 4:25–26), *her* Messiah.

Just then, the disciples returned and marveled that He had been speaking with a Samaritan woman. The woman seized the opportunity to spread the word about Jesus in the city: "From that city many of the Samaritans believed in Him because of the word of the woman who testified, 'He told me all the things that I have done'" (4:39). How do we know this woman was changed? Her life reflected the evidence. Her testimony brought the city's inhabitants out to meet Christ. The result? The woman and many other Samaritans placed their faith in Jesus as the Messiah (4:41–42).

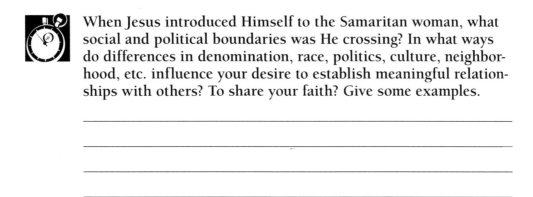

When Jesus introduced Himself to the Samaritan woman, what social and political boundaries was He crossing? In what ways do differences in denomination, race, politics, culture, neighborhood, etc. influence your desire to establish meaningful relationships with others? To share your faith? Give some examples.

Notice that, though He knew all the woman's sins, Jesus did not follow up His conversation with, "Clean up your act, and then you can believe." How does this challenge or affirm your concept of God's character?

_____

_____

_____

_____

Do you find yourself putting conditions on others before you extend Jesus's love to them? Name a few examples. Determine today to release these situations to God, letting Him do His work of change in their lives. Write your prayer below.

_____

_____

_____

_____

A Blind Beggar

On another occasion, Jesus and His disciples came across a beggar who had been blind since birth. Rather than reaching out to this man with compassion, the disciples used his plight as a springboard for raising a theological question:

> And His disciples asked Him, "Rabbi, who sinned, this man or his parents, that he would be born blind?" (John 9:2)

Perhaps the disciples had grown callous toward beggars because these disabled and disadvantaged people were such a common and despised sight in Palestine. Jesus answered the disciples' query, saying:

> It was neither that this man sinned, nor his parents; but it was so that the works of God might be displayed in him. (9:3)

Illustrating the truth of His statement, Jesus mercifully chose to heal the blind man.

Read John 9:6–11. What methods did Jesus use to heal the man of his blindness?

_____

_____

_____

_____

How does the use of clay here relate to the idea of the potter we studied earlier? What conclusions about Jesus's identity can we draw from these images?

_____

_____

_____

_____

This man's healing caused quite a sensation. Many of the beggar's neighbors and acquaintances couldn't believe that he was the same man. When he reassured them of his identity and explained how Jesus had healed him, they took him before the Pharisees. The beggar's testimony sparked a controversy among the religious leaders concerning who Jesus was. Regardless of what the beggar said, however, the Pharisees refused to believe that he had ever been blind.

In an attempt to settle the issue, the religious authorities summoned the man's parents. His parents identified the beggar as their son and confirmed that he had been born blind. But, because they were afraid of being excommunicated from the synagogue, they did not support their son's story of healing. Yet even their cowardice did not thwart their son's persistence. In fact, the beggar argued openly with the Pharisees, contending that his miraculous healing provided ample evidence that Jesus came from God (John 9:18–27).

In John 9:35–41, Jesus sought out the blind man, who had been excommunicated from the synagogue by the religious leaders. From this context, why do you think He did so?

_____

_____

_____

_____

Consider Jesus's response to the Pharisees in John 9:40–41. What did He mean when He said, "Since you say 'we see,' your sin remains"?

_____

_____

_____

_____

What parable did Jesus tell immediately after this one (see John 10)? What is significant about this parable in the context of the blind man's healing and the Pharisees' protests?

_____

_____

_____

_____

A Doubting Disciple

During Jesus's earthly ministry, the disciple Thomas showed his commitment to Christ by expressing his willingness to die with Him (John 11:16). After Jesus was crucified and placed in the tomb, however, Thomas was grieved and felt greatly disillusioned. When Thomas heard the other disciples report that they had seen Jesus alive again, he refused to believe them. He said that personally seeing the crucified Christ alive would be the only way to resolve his deep-seated doubt (20:25).

Several days later, Christ reappeared to the disciples, and this time Thomas was with them. Jesus produced the evidence Thomas needed, allowing the grieving disciple to place his hands in the nail wounds. Thomas then responded by expressing faith in Christ as His Lord and God (20:28). Once more, Jesus broke down the walls that separated Him from someone who needed Him, and once again, He changed a life for eternity.

In Case You Were Wondering

Q: I've prayed over and over again for God to take away a particular sin in my life, but I keep falling into the same sin. Does this mean that my heart hasn't truly been changed?

A: While we as believers will still commit some sins after we accept Christ, our lives should not be carnal or controlled by negative sin patterns. We're no longer in bondage to sin or our fleshly desires. God has granted us the ability to exercise wisdom, discernment, self-control, and discipline as the Holy Spirit guides our thoughts, words, and actions.

Knowing Scripture, being accountable to others, and practicing daily spiritual disciplines are some of the best ways to arm ourselves against dangerous sin patterns. The daily practice of the spiritual life is part of the means by which believers are able to more intimately know their God, relate to and rest in their new life in Christ, and experience true spiritual change and liberation from life-dominating patterns of sin. The spiritual disciplines promote growth in our devotion to God and our ability to grasp, personalize, believe, and apply Scripture to our lives.

Assembling together weekly with other believers for accountability, fellowship, worship, ministry, prayer, and the teaching of God's Word is also vital to our spiritual health. The Holy Spirit does not operate in a mindless vacuum devoid of God's point of view. The Word and the Spirit work together so that if we fail to take time to be alone with God and His Word, two things will happen: (a) we will quench the ministry of the Spirit and grieve Him, and (b) we will be influenced and deceived by the negative attitudes and ungodly viewpoints of the world around us.

Our heavenly Father may allow *trials* in our lives, but He will never *tempt* us to sin. James wrote:

> Let no one say when he is tempted, "I am being tempted by God"; for God cannot be tempted by evil, and He Himself does not tempt anyone. But each one is tempted when he is carried away and enticed by his own lust. Then when lust has conceived, it gives birth to sin; and when sin is accomplished, it brings forth death. (James 1:13–15)

See the progression? Sin and temptation are part of an insidious process by which our fleshly lusts and desires lead to sin and our sin, ultimately, leads to spiritual death. But God's power triumphs over both Satan's power and the power of our own desires. God's Word promises us that, "No temptation has overtaken you but such as is common to man; and God is faithful, who will not allow you to be tempted beyond what you are able, but with the temptation will provide the way of escape also, so that you will be able to endure it" (1 Corinthians 10:13).

Paul wrote, "If anyone is in Christ, he is a new creature; the old things passed away; behold, new things have come" (2 Corinthians 5:17). When we look at the delicate finery of a butterfly's wings, we find it hard to believe that this exquisite creature was once an ugly caterpillar crawling around in the dirt. You've experienced spiritual metamorphosis; you're a new creature. Are you living like it?

The same Lord who changed the lives of an immoral Samaritan woman, a blind beggar, and a skeptical disciple is committed to changing you. He will not give up on you. However, you can either cooperate with Him or resist His work in your life. If you are fighting Him, will you yield and submit to Him today? He desires to give you only the best, so relax and let Him have His way. Let the Potter shape you into a useful vessel. Let the Sculptor chip away at the rough edges so He can create the beautiful image He desires. Remember: Changing lives is Jesus's business.

The Holy Spirit

10

THE SPIRIT WHO IS NOT A GHOST

John 16:1–15

Something that we can't see, smell, touch, or taste helps keep us alive. It can also cool us down on a hot day, dry out a flooded field, forcefully overturn a ship, and topple a tall building.

What is this mysterious force? Air. Though we can't see it, air provides useful, powerful, and essential elements to our lives. It's always at work behind the scenes. In much the same way, the Holy Spirit moves in our lives. Author J. I. Packer wrote:

> Power in action is in fact the basic biblical thought whenever God's Spirit is mentioned. . . .
>
> The [biblical] picture [of the Holy Spirit] is of air made to move vigorously, even violently, and the thought that the picture expresses is of energy let loose, executive force invading, power in exercise, life demonstrated by activity.[1]

What a powerful description of the Holy Spirit and His work! The Spirit may be invisible, but He's no ghost. He's living, active, and able to move in the lives of believers and non-believers alike.

Getting to the Root

The Bible uses the same words to refer to the Holy Spirit as it does to refer to air. The Hebrew word *ruach* and the Greek term *pneuma* may be translated "air," "breath," "wind," or "spirit."[2]

In what ways is the Holy Spirit similar to air? What are the nuanced differences between the air, a breath, the wind, and the Holy Spirit of God?

_____

_____

_____

_____

WHAT THE HOLY SPIRIT IS AND IS NOT

In some churches, the Holy Spirit is rarely mentioned, while in other congregations, He's the sole center of attention and focus of worship. Both extremes have led to erroneous ideas concerning the person and work of the Spirit, so let's take a fresh look as we consider what Scripture has to say about Him.

First, *the Holy Spirit is not an "it" but a person.* Author A. W. Tozer wrote:

Spell this out in capital letters: THE HOLY SPIRIT IS A PERSON. He is not enthusiasm. He is not courage. He is not energy. He is not the personification of all good qualities, like Jack Frost is the personification of cold weather. Actually, the Holy Spirit is not the personification of anything. . . . He has individuality. He is one being and not another. He has will and intelligence. He has hearing. He has knowledge and sympathy and ability to love and see and think. He can hear, speak, desire, grieve and rejoice. He is a Person.[3]

Some people reject the concept of the Holy Spirit as a real person. They may consider Him an impersonal force, an ethereal substance, or even simply a "life principle" that guides our actions. The Bible, however, makes the truth clear. Scripture attributes to the Holy Spirit action, movement, intelligence, understanding, and will—all of which are characteristics of rational beings (1 Corinthians 2:10–11; 12:11). The Bible's description of the Holy Spirit's activities also emphasizes His personhood. For instance, He creates, empowers, teaches, guides, intercedes, and comforts (Genesis 1:2; Job 33:4; Zechariah 4:6; Luke 1:35; John 14:26; Acts 1:8; Romans 8:26–27). Such evidence makes it plain that the Holy Spirit is truly one of the three persons of the Godhead.

 Most likely, you've encountered people with misguided ideas and beliefs about the person and work of the Spirit. Some tend to elevate the Spirit and minimize the work of the Father and Son, while others completely deny the existence or work of the Spirit. Where do you think these ideas came from? Why do you think that many people tend to misunderstand who the Holy Spirit is?

Second, *the Holy Spirit is not passive, but active and involved.* Before Christ's betrayal and death, He told His disciples that His eventual departure would be to their advantage. He assured them that when He left, "the Helper"—the Holy Spirit—would come to them (John 16:7). What would this Helper do when He came? Jesus said that the Spirit would convict the world concerning sin, righteousness, and judgment; guide the disciples into all truth; and glorify Christ (16:8, 13–14). Jesus promised that the Holy Spirit also would enable Christians to spread the gospel worldwide (Acts 1:8). We can see this promise being fulfilled today in virtually every tribe and nation. Now, that's involvement!

Have you personally experienced the helping work of the Holy Spirit? If so, how? Give one or more concrete examples. Compare your examples with the Spirit's role discussed earlier.

_____

_____

_____

_____

Third, *the Holy Spirit is not imaginary, but real and relevant.* We've all heard the old adage, "Seeing is believing." Beneath this saying lies the assumption that everything *real* is visible, but this assumption is not always true. For example, we cannot see the wind, but we can observe and experience its tangible effects. We can't see attributes like truth, purity, love, or wisdom, but we know they exist, and we can perceive and measure their influence in our lives and in the lives of others. Likewise, we cannot view the Holy Spirit with our eyes, but we can see the results of His work, both within ourselves and all over the world.

Last, *the Holy Spirit is not less than God, but fully God.* As the third person of the Godhead, the Holy Spirit is equal to the Father and the Son in every aspect of deity because He shares their divine essence. The Bible tells us this in numerous places, but perhaps the clearest evidence appears in Acts 5. Here, the apostle Peter confronts Ananias and Sapphira and calls them to take responsibility for their deceitful actions. He asks Ananias, "Why has Satan filled your heart to lie to the Holy Spirit . . . ?" (5:3). Peter then adds, "You have not lied to men, but to God" (5:4). Lying to the Holy Spirit means lying to deity, because the Spirit is God and no less.

Why do people tend to think of the Holy Spirit as "less than" God the Father and God the Son? In which ways have the church and culture perpetuated this view?

_____

_____

_____

_____

Have you struggled to identify the Spirit yourself? If so, in what ways and situations?

_____

_____

_____

_____

WHY THE HOLY SPIRIT IS HERE

On the eve of Christ's death, Jesus told His disciples that He would soon return to the Father. He also let them know in no uncertain terms that they would be despised and killed because of their commitment to Him.

These revelations grieved the disciples. They had expected Jesus, the long-awaited Messiah, to overthrow the Roman government and establish a world order of peace, prosperity, and justice. But now, that belief was shattered. The disciples saw that their King planned to leave them.

Sensing their sorrow, Christ sought to comfort His band of followers by telling them about a wonderful Helper who would aid them once Jesus ascended to heaven. How could this be so? Well, for one thing, the Holy Spirit could be present everywhere at once, while Jesus, in His humanity, could not because of the limitations of His physical body. Furthermore, the invisibility of the Spirit would help strengthen the disciples' faith by calling them to trust in something they could not see. After all, isn't it usually easier to trust in what can be seen rather than in what cannot? But God often calls on us to believe in the invisible and in that which is not yet fulfilled. He knows that this is how our faith deepens.

 ## In Case You Were Wondering

Q: How do I know for certain that the Holy Spirit is guiding me, rather than my own thoughts, desires, or even demonic deception?

A: The inner promptings of the Holy Spirit can seem, well, very *mysterious.* They cannot be nailed down and dissected with precision; however, they also cannot be denied. Many in God's family have sensed some inner promptings at one time or another. How do we handle them? Take to heart just a couple of suggestions.

First, *even when you feel certain a prompting is from the Spirit, tread softly.* Begin by using the Scriptures as your guide. The Lord doesn't lead us to do or say anything that would contradict His revealed Word. Even the devil quoted Scripture to Jesus—and twisted it. So if the promptings are of the Lord, they won't contradict anything that the Bible says or means. Seek counsel from other mature believers, for "where there is no guidance the people fall, but in abundance of counselors there is victory" (Proverbs 11:14). In addition, peace will remain your companion, because the fruit of the Spirit is peace (Galatians 5:22).

Second, *when you sense that the direction is of God, move forward, but humbly allow God to redirect any misunderstanding on your part.* Ultimately, the best way to know something is God's will is in hindsight. But you can pray, "Lord, it really seems from Scripture, from counsel, and from the leanings of my heart, You are leading me this direction. But I want to remain aware of the fact I can be deceived even by my own heart (Jeremiah 17:9). As I move in this direction, please guide me, for all I want is to glorify you."

Above all, continue to seek after God. He promises to illuminate His Word to us and guide us with His Spirit. Remember, the Spirit's role is to guide us in truth, not confusion.

WHAT THE HOLY SPIRIT DOES

On that same fateful evening, Jesus went on to tell His disciples what the Holy Spirit would do once He came to earth.

Among Non-Christians

Jesus focused first on the Spirit's work in the lives of the unsaved. He said that God's Spirit would "convict the world concerning sin, . . . because they do not believe in Me" (John 16:8–9). He also said that the Spirit would "convict the world concerning righteousness, because I go to the Father and you no longer see Me" (16:8, 10).

The Greek word translated *convict* means, "to pronounce a judicial verdict by which the guilt of the culprit at the bar of justice is defined and fixed."[4] The Holy Spirit acts as a divine prosecuting attorney, demonstrating to us that we do not measure up to God's perfect moral standard.

Judgment is the logical consequence of standing guilty before God. Once we learn that our thoughts and actions fall short of Christ's righteousness, we gain a realistic sense of our own sinfulness and recognize that without the sacrifice of Christ, we would face utter condemnation. Even Satan, the wicked spiritual ruler of earth, realizes that his fate is sealed. His goal is to do as much harm to God's people as he can in the meantime.

We all feel the conviction of the Spirit, both before and after we choose to become Christians. We may call it something else, and we may try to stifle the Spirit's work in our hearts or drown out His still, small voice with television, movies, exercise, hobbies, relationships, travel, education, philosophy, and other pursuits. We may try to escape the Spirit's conviction through alcohol, drugs, gambling, Internet pornography, or sexual addictions. But we'll never be able to erase the gnawing conviction that whispers in our inmost being: "You're lost. You're separated from God. You're a sinner. On your own, you're guilty and without hope. You need Christ." We can't run away from the truth we know, and God has placed a responsive spirit within us that can only be satisfied in Him.

Among Christians

Jesus also promised that the Holy Spirit would guide believers further along the path of truth as it is embodied in Christ. The Spirit has accomplished this by inspiring the New Testament, the last written revelation of God to man. Today, the Holy Spirit illuminates the content and application of the Scriptures, and He uses the Word and our circumstances to mature us into Christlikeness. In all these things, the Spirit's central goal is to glorify Christ, not Himself. The Spirit's role is to magnify the Father and the Son and to empower those who desire to faithfully worship the Father in spirit and in truth.

Digging Deeper

The Holy Spirit's conviction can remove the stress many believers feel with regard to evangelism. We who are Christians need not convince people that they're sinners. That's the Holy Spirit's job! But we do have the joyful responsibility of sharing the gospel with others, perhaps offering them our testimony of how God has changed our lives and given us eternal life through His Son, Jesus Christ. Then, we must trust God with the results. The outcome of our evangelism is His responsibility, not ours. Only God converts.

Have you ever felt led by the Spirit to share the gospel with someone? If so, what was your response, and what happened as a result?

_____

_____

_____

_____

PRACTICAL TRUTHS CONCERNING THE HOLY SPIRIT'S WORK

Reflecting on the identity and activity of the Holy Spirit, we can recognize at least four practical truths concerning His work in our lives.

1. Because the Spirit is a person, we experience Him as He heals our relationships. The Holy Spirit prompts us to interact with others, to show them love, to offer them grace, and to forgive them, even when we may not feel like doing so in our selfishness.

2. Because He is active and involved, we experience the Spirit comforting us in our sorrows and guiding us in our pursuits. We can sense Him nudging us toward (or away from) particular thoughts, words, or actions. The Spirit's promptings will always be in line with God's Word.

3. Because He is real and relevant, we experience Him giving us power and perseverance. As we submit to His work in our lives, He fills us and empowers us to live as He desires, experiencing peace, purpose, and joy.

4. Because He is God, we experience Him as He controls our circumstances and transforms our lives. He gives us the spiritual discernment we need to be able to walk away from dangerous, compromising situations. The Spirit is constantly at work in our lives—speaking to us, comforting us, guiding us, and molding us into the image of Jesus Christ.

How do you experience the empowering work of the Holy Spirit in your day-to-day life?

_____

_____

_____

_____

If there's a particular time in your life when the Spirit powerfully and unmistakably directed you in a certain way, write about it here. How did this experience change you?

_____

_____

_____

_____

Like the wind, the Holy Spirit moves when and where God has ordained—often mysteriously, but always within the realm of biblical truth. Take time now to say or write out a prayer to God, thanking Him for sending the Spirit to live within you, comfort you, and guide you in your daily walk with Christ.

_____

_____

_____

_____

To close, read or sing the lyrics of the following song, "Spirit of the Living God." Also take a few moments to pray that you will be sensitive to the Holy Spirit who, like a breath of fresh air, will rejuvenate your soul and continue to guide you in your walk with God.

Spirit of the Living God,
Fall afresh on me.
Spirit of the Living God,
Fall afresh on me.
Melt me, mold me,
Fill me, use me.
Spirit of the Living God,
Fall afresh on me.[5]

THE DEPRAVITY OF HUMANITY

11

From Creation to Corruption

Selected Scriptures

Have you ever considered the enormous significance of creation as the very first act recorded in the Bible? Genesis 1:1 tells us, "In the beginning God *created* the heavens and the earth" (emphasis added). In the Hebrew language, the writer placed the verb before the subject to emphasize Yahweh's powerful action: "In the beginning *created* Elohim the heavens and the earth."

On the sixth and final day of creation, God celebrated His crowning achievement, forming humans in His own image, according to Genesis 1:26–27. And as He surveyed His creation, the Father declared it to be "very good" (1:31). As humans, we reflect the exquisite design and imaginative spark that the Almighty used to create the world, and this spark of creative genius represents one of the vital aspects of our being that separates us from every other created thing.

 Getting to the Root

The Hebrew word *bara* used in the book of Genesis means "to create, shape, bring about, make or produce."[1] In Scripture, this form of the word refers to God's activity of creating *ex nihilo*, which means "out of nothing." As humans, we do not create *ex nihilo*, but we do have the ability to rearrange our existing, comfortable patterns of thinking, acting, and expressing ourselves in order to infuse our spiritual lives with a fresh burst of creativity and a renewed commitment to our relationships with God and others.

Although modern science was originally established by individuals who believed Genesis 1:1, the rise of the Enlightenment and the ensuing development of Darwinian evolutionary theory have led the scientific community away from its biblical moorings. However, several recent discoveries have caused some scientists to consider a return to the truth of the Bible's portrayal of the origin of the universe and the beginning of life. For example, two of Britain's most distinguished scientists have argued that the probable chance of life arising from purely inorganic and natural processes is 1 in 10 to the 40,000th power—a number greater than the estimated number of atoms in the universe! Clearly, life did not occur on Earth by random chance. We only have to look around at the exquisite, detailed beauty of nature to understand that creating life required God's divine intelligence and supernatural design.

Let's focus our attention now on Genesis 1–3. The emphasis in this passage of Scripture soon turns from the creation of the universe and all it contains to the creation and fall of mankind.

MANKIND'S ROLE IN RULING CREATION

Throughout Genesis 1, God created living things and told them to reproduce "after their own kind" (1:11–12, 21, 24–25). This phrase indicates that new life forms were created directly by God and replicated after that which produced them; they did not evolve from a common ancestor. It also suggests that the creatures He made were distinct from one another and would maintain their uniqueness throughout all succeeding generations. 1 Corinthians 15:39 states: "All flesh is not the same flesh, but there is one flesh of men, and another flesh of beasts, and another flesh of birds, and another of fish."

We share some characteristics with other creatures, but we differ from them in that we are the only creation made in the image of God. We can't ignore the physical, emotional, spiritual, and rational distinctions between animals and people. God created Adam and Eve to be His visible representatives and rulers on earth (Genesis 1:28), and we, as their descendants, have the same responsibility.

Digging Deeper

The Image of God (*Imago Dei*)

What does the phrase *the image of God* mean? Theologians have wrestled long and hard with this question because the answer to it impacts how we think about Christ's saving work, Christian ethics, and other important spiritual matters. Some have argued that *image* refers to man's capacity to rule, because ruling is mentioned in connection with the image in Genesis 1:26. Some have argued that the image relates to personal knowledge of God. Still others argue that it relates to morality, righteousness, and holiness (Ephesians 4:24). Finally, some have suggested that the image of God relates to man's capacity for an intimate relationship with God.

The truth probably lies in a combination of these. The ways in which men and women are like God and the attributes that we share with Him are what compose His image within us. Yet we must also recognize the clear distinctions between our limited human selves and our holy, all-powerful, and omniscient God.

HOW CORRUPTION BEGAN

God created Adam as the first human being, placed him in the Garden of Eden, and told him to cultivate and keep it. Then "The Lord God commanded the man, saying, 'From any tree of the garden you may eat freely; but from the tree of the knowledge of good and evil you shall not eat, for in the day that you eat from it you will surely die'" (Genesis 2:16–17).

Genesis 2:4–25 expands on what chapter one tells us about the creation of man. Read Genesis 2:4–7. From what did God create man? What did He breathe into his nostrils?

_____

_____

_____

_____

Some time later, God formed Eve. Read Genesis 2:18. Why did God create the woman?

_____

_____

_____

According to Genesis 2:21–22, *how* did God create Eve?

_____

_____

_____

_____

Read Genesis 2:23–25. How would you describe the spiritual, emotional, and physical intimacy that the man and the woman shared at this point?

_____

_____

_____

_____

Unfortunately, this beautiful garden scene quickly grew ugly. Through the tragic abuse of their God-given freedom, Adam and Eve gave in to temptation and ate from the forbidden tree (Genesis 3:1–6). The punishment that followed was exactly the penalty that God had warned them about—death.

Scripture explains physical death not as the end of a person's existence, but as separation from the physical body. When a person dies, his or her soul and spirit separate from the physical body (John 19:30; 2 Corinthians 5:1–8). In the case of a person who does not have a relationship with God, death also means eternal separation from the Lord and eternal retribution for sin. Theologians call this "spiritual death" (Romans 6:23).

Although Adam and Eve did not experience immediate physical death, their sin initiated the degeneration process that would lead to their demise (Genesis 3:19). In other ways, they did experience a separation—or spiritual death—right after they sinned. According to Genesis 3:8, the open fellowship they had enjoyed with God and each other was marred. Their perfect marital intimacy was also lost. No longer could they enjoy each other's presence "naked and unashamed" (Genesis 2:25). They felt shame and became preoccupied with protecting themselves from each other, hiding behind clothing and blaming each other rather than taking responsibility for their own sin (Genesis 3:7, 9–13).

In addition to the consequences of immediate spiritual death and eventual physical death, Adam and Eve forfeited their control over the earth. The land that had been submissive to their rule suddenly became a source of conflict and arduous labor (3:17–19). The vicious circle of corruption had begun, and it would not remain confined to the Garden of Eden (3:23–24). It would spread throughout the earth and all of mankind.

Two Truths about Creation

From the Genesis passages, we can glean two truths about creation. First, *mankind is unique.* Only humankind, *homo sapiens,* has been created in God's image, bearing His divine likeness and His unique creative signature.

Second, we can glean from multiple references in Scripture that *mankind is different from and superior to the animals.* God didn't tell any other species to take charge of creation; He told humans to take charge of it. In Genesis 1:26,

God said, "Let them (man and woman) rule . . . over all the earth." The vivid Hebrew verb for *rule, radah*, means, "to have dominion, rule, dominate, prevail, or subdue."[2] This word has an active, powerful connotation. God created man and woman as superior to the animals, and He expected Adam and Eve to have dominion over them.

WHERE CORRUPTION LEADS

Once they chose to sin against God, Adam and Eve's natures were corrupted. We call this *depravity*. This does not mean that they were as *bad* as they could be, but it does mean that, positionally, they were as *bad off* as they could be. They had been alienated from God, from the world they lived in, from each other, and even from their former innocence. Sin had polluted their lives. And, to make matters worse, Adam and Eve passed this disease on to their children. For instance, one of their sons, Cain, manifested some of the worst symptoms of depravity when he maliciously murdered his brother Abel in cold blood (Genesis 4:1–8).

Obviously, men and women, once bearing the perfect image of God, now bore a marred image—that of sinful man, passed down from Adam. In fact, Genesis 5:3 says specifically that Adam's son Seth was conceived in the image of his father. Though man did not completely lose the divine image in which he was created, he now also reflected the depravity brought on by Adam and Eve's sin. The remainder of Scripture records the tragic march of corruption through human history. This spiritual disease is so pervasive and devastating that the apostle Paul penned these words regarding the human condition:

> Both Jews and Greeks are all under sin; as it is written,
> "There is none righteous, not even one;
> There is none who understands,
> There is none who seeks for God;
> All have turned aside, together they have become useless;
> There is none who does good,
> There is not even one." (Romans 3:9–12)

What This Means for Us

The bottom line is that all of us suffer from the same disease—sinful depravity. Read Romans 6:23. What are the wages of sin?

_____

_____

What are some ways in which you can see your fallen nature manifested in your life?

_____

_____

_____

_____

What is the free gift of God?

_____

_____

Is there no escape? Are we all doomed? Mercifully, no. God offered up His only Son, Jesus Christ, to provide us with a way out of our corruption and into renewed wholeness and a restored relationship with God. Jesus chose to take our death sentence upon Himself and exchange it for life, which He compassionately makes available to us. All we have to do is accept it! The apostle Paul explained the righteous transaction this way:

> For if by the transgression of the one, death reigned through the one, much more those who receive the abundance of grace and of the gift of righteousness will reign in life through the One, Jesus Christ. (Romans 5:17)

When we place our trust in Jesus Christ and acknowledge His payment for our depravity, we are saved from the _penalty_ of sin. As He changes our hearts by the work of His Spirit, we experience freedom from the _power_ of sin. When we finally pass from this life on earth into eternity with God, we'll be saved from the _presence_ of sin. And once we've broken the strongholds of the penalty, the power, and the presence of sin, we have complete salvation from corruption! Unlike Humpty Dumpty, we _can_ be put back together again because of all that Christ has done for us. Creating a parody of the popular nursery rhyme, we could describe our position this way:

Jesus came to our wall;
Jesus Christ died for our fall.
He slew Queen Death.
He crushed King Sin.
Through grace He put us together again.

In Case You Were Wondering

Q: I feel like I'm under spiritual oppression or attack. What can I do?

A: Whether you're a new believer or a mature follower of Christ, you may not realize a very important truth—you are a soldier in an ongoing war. This reality is not the philosophical struggle between good and evil, but part of an ancient rebellion between the forces of Satan and the Almighty God. Thankfully, there's no comparison between the awesome power and limitless knowledge of the Almighty and Satan's opposition, which is doomed to fail. The battle is progressing according to God's plan, and God will win in the end.

Spiritual forces that we cannot see affect our world by waging constant battle in and around human society. On one side are Satan and his demonic forces. One-third of the angels rebelled against God under the leadership of Satan and became what Scripture refers to as demons. Satan and his demons do have power; their goal is to harass, attack, tempt, and corrupt Christians, prevent conversions, and dishonor God (Ephesians 6:11–12).

On the other side of the eternal conflict are God and His holy angels. These angels are perfect, sinless, and extremely powerful. These ministering spirits carry out God's plan and work for the benefit and protection of His people.

Satan and his demons operate in the kingdom of darkness and sin. When we live in unconfessed sin, we give the devil a foothold; an opportunity to harden our hearts, hinder our walk with Christ, and all but extinguish our productive witness for the Lord. Satan constantly accuses us of sin, but in light of the definitive break with sin that Christ obtained for His people, Satan's accusations are powerless and unable to permanently separate us from God. The more we grow in sanctification and holiness, the stronger we become against Satan's temptations.

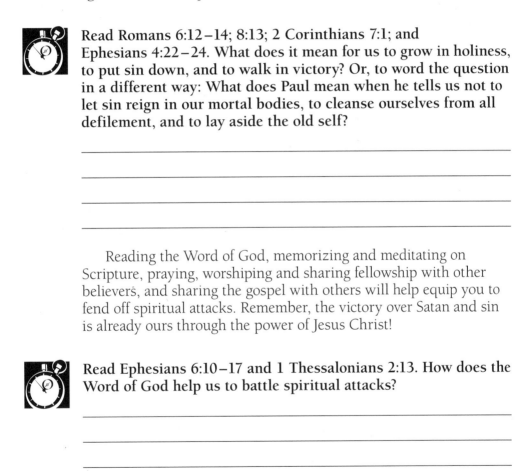

Read Romans 6:12–14; 8:13; 2 Corinthians 7:1; and Ephesians 4:22–24. What does it mean for us to grow in holiness, to put sin down, and to walk in victory? Or, to word the question in a different way: What does Paul mean when he tells us not to let sin reign in our mortal bodies, to cleanse ourselves from all defilement, and to lay aside the old self?

_____

_____

_____

_____

Reading the Word of God, memorizing and meditating on Scripture, praying, worshiping and sharing fellowship with other believers, and sharing the gospel with others will help equip you to fend off spiritual attacks. Remember, the victory over Satan and sin is already ours through the power of Jesus Christ!

Read Ephesians 6:10–17 and 1 Thessalonians 2:13. How does the Word of God help us to battle spiritual attacks?

_____

_____

_____

Faith is not an offensive weapon—we do not use faith to claim victory or to declare dominance. Our shield of faith is defensive—when the enemy accuses us, when flaming arrows are hurled at us, we prevail over the attack by our faith in Christ (Ephesians 6:16). When all seems lost, we "walk by faith, not by sight." Our offensive weapons are the sword of the Spirit, which is the Word of God, and prayer. The truth of the Word of God overcomes strongholds in the heart and mind, and prayer places the battle where it belongs—with God.

THE GOOD NEWS

Because of Christ's work in our lives, our story has a happy ending. Though our lives have been marred by sin, Jesus has "unscrambled the egg" of Humpty Dumpty and put us back together again. He has picked up the pieces of our shattered lives and brought us healing and restoration. Wherever sin appears, there must be a sinner. And wherever there's a sinner, there's a Savior.

12

EXPOSING THE DARK SIDE
Selected Scriptures

Everyone loves good news! Most of us prefer to maximize the positive aspects of life and minimize the negative. But the good news found in the Word of God makes up only *part* of the message of Christianity. When we stop to think about it, we can't truly appreciate God's grace and the abundant life we have in Christ until we fully understand the dark, dismal backdrop of our humanity and sin. We must recognize the dark side of our nature, which we prefer to keep hidden from public view.

Back in 1886, Robert Louis Stevenson wrote a classic story called *Dr. Jekyll and Mr. Hyde* that reflected the two sides of human nature. He and Mark Twain lived during the same time period, so maybe it was Stevenson's tale that prompted Twain to quip: "Everyone is a moon and has a dark side which he never shows to anybody." [1]

Jesus reflected the truth of this sentiment thousands of years earlier when He sternly opposed the hypocrisy of the Pharisees and scribes:

> Woe to you, scribes and Pharisees, hypocrites! For you are like whitewashed tombs which on the outside appear beautiful, but inside they are full of dead men's bones and all uncleanness. So you, too, outwardly appear righteous to men, but inwardly you are full of hypocrisy and lawlessness. (Matthew 23:27–28)

Let's not kid ourselves that the "dark side" was a problem only for the Pharisees. Take a few moments to stop and think how you've lived your life over the past several days. You may have behaved rather well externally, but probably not as well internally! What thoughts, impulses, drives, and motives prompted the actions that you lived out? Were these inner thoughts obvious, or did you keep them hidden?

A few of your underlying motivations may have surfaced, but you probably tried your best to keep your dark side hidden and show your "good side" while in public. We all do; it's part of our fallen human nature!

In what ways have you tried to keep your "dark side" hidden from others? In which places or contexts do you feel the most pressure to "put up a good front"? Why?

_____

_____

_____

_____

In which places or contexts (or around which people) do you feel that you can really relax and be yourself? Why do you think this is the case?

_____

_____

_____

_____

DEPRAVITY DEFINED AND EXPLAINED

What's the deadliest killer of humanity? Believe it or not, it's not heart disease or cancer—it's depravity. Depravity infests our lives, and we all suffer from its consequences. And to make matters worse, we pass our sinfulness and depravity on to each subsequent generation (Genesis 3).

In your own words, how would you define the concept of depravity?

_____

_____

_____

Now, look up Mark 7:20–23; Luke 4:18; John 8:31–36; and Romans 3:10–18; 5:12; 6:16–18. How do these passages expand your understanding of human depravity?

_____

_____

_____

_____

 ### Getting to the Root

In Hebrew, the word for depravity, *shachatah*, is derived from the root *shachat*, which means "to slaughter or beat" (Hosea 5:2). Hosea 9:9 contains the word *shachath*, a variant of the same term meaning "to go to ruin; to act corruptly."[2]

Paul uses the Greek term *adokimos* in Romans 1:28 to mean *depraved*. This term is also translated as "not standing the test; rejected; disqualified; unapproved; worthless."[3]

The Bible describes mankind's depraved condition in a variety of ways. It tells us that we're enslaved to sin and need to be set free. We're sick with sin and in need of healing. We're impoverished by sin and in need of God's riches. The Scriptures also say that mankind is polluted by sin and needs to be cleansed. We're blinded by sin and need restored sight. We're lost in sin's darkness and need Christ's light to illuminate our path. We're dead in our sin and desperately in need of fresh, revitalized, and abundant life.

These descriptions graphically illustrate the destructive, degenerative nature of depravity. All humans suffer corruption, and that corruption affects us physically, emotionally, mentally, spiritually, and relationally. The corruption of humanity through sin is called "total depravity." As we mentioned previously, this doctrine does not mean mankind is as *bad* as we could be, but that we are as *bad off* as we could be. In other words, we have no way, on our own, of commending ourselves to God.

Genesis 6:5 contains one of the most telling statements in all of Scripture regarding the depravity of humanity:

> Then the Lord saw that the wickedness of man was great on the earth, and that *every intent of the thoughts of his heart was only evil continually.* (emphasis added)

"Every intent . . . was only evil continually." This verse describes an inescapable universal cesspool within all humanity—a hidden source of pollution that lies at the root of wrong. And it exists in the soul of every person!

Psalm 51 also helps us to come to terms with the doctrine of depravity. David wrote this psalm following Nathan's confrontation with him after the king's adultery-murder scandal involving Bathsheba and her husband, Uriah:

> Be gracious to me, O God, according to Your lovingkindness;
> According to the greatness of Your compassion
>   blot out my transgressions.
> Wash me thoroughly from my iniquity
> And cleanse me from my sin.
> For I know my transgressions,
> And my sin is ever before me.
> Against You, You only, I have sinned
> And done what is evil in Your sight,
> So that You are justified when You speak
> And blameless when You judge. (Psalm 51:1–4)

What words does David use to refer to his sin in Psalm 51:1–4?

_____

_____

_____

_____

What is his plea in this psalm? How would you describe his heart's attitude and his position before God?

_____

_____

_____

_____

David begins this psalm with a desperate plea for grace, which shouldn't surprise us. The only way David could expect to survive was by the grace of God. That's the only way *any* of us can survive! But what *is* grace, exactly? How would you define it?

_____

_____

_____

_____

Perhaps the simplest and best-known definition of grace is "unmerited favor when we deserve wrath." God's grace involves the merciful and loving acts that He does for us that we don't deserve, we can't earn, and we'll never be able to repay. On our own, we're lost in our sinfulness, helpless to change, and polluted to the core. All we can do is cry out for grace! God's unmerited favor is our only hope. We're all depraved, unable to do anything on our own merit to please God. We've all received the penalty of sin, judgment, and death. Only Christ can redeem us from death and renew us to deep fellowship and proper standing before our heavenly Father so that we may have eternal life with Him.

How have you experienced God's grace in your life with regard to your sin?

_____

_____

_____

_____

HUMANITY SURVEYED AND EXPOSED

The Bible tells us the truth about its heroes and heroines in the faith. Unlike *Vogue* magazine, Scripture doesn't airbrush its character portraits! When it depicts its heroes and heroines, it reveals them as they really are—warts, scars, insecurities, failures, and all. Whenever we're tempted to elevate a biblical man or woman to a pedestal of worship, one of his or her sinful acts, attitudes, or confessions brings each one down to size. Each character is completely, totally, and thoroughly human, and every last one (except Jesus) possesses a sinful nature like ours.

Now, let's take a look at five biblical characters and see how their humanity revealed itself in their attitudes, their actions, and their choices.

Noah

Remember the passage from Genesis 6:5 that we read earlier in the chapter? It described the earth and its surroundings at the time of Noah. The Lord was grieved that He had made man. Before judging and destroying humanity by sending the flood, He surveyed the world, looking for one person who would qualify as righteous. Sadly, there was only one man, Noah, who found favor in God's sight. Scripture says this about Noah:

> These are the records of the generations of Noah. Noah was a righteous man, blameless in his time; Noah walked with God. (Genesis 6:9)

Noah was righteous; he was blameless; he walked with God. That's quite a resume! This godly man was surrounded by gross wickedness, like a flower growing out of a cesspool. God appointed him to build the ark in order to save his family from drowning in the flood. And that's exactly what Noah did. He worked on it consistently for 120 years, enduring constant ridicule from those around him. But while he worked, he preached. And while he preached, he warned people about the flood. When he finally finished the ark, he ushered his family inside, and then the flood began. Only Noah and his family were saved from destruction.

Genesis 9 brings us to the end of the flood, when Noah and his family disembark from the ark and settle onto a "new" earth. Here stands a man who has been walking with God for all these years. What a model of courage and determination! But as soon as we're about to see Noah as a flawless, godly man, we find out that he has a dark side.

> Then Noah began farming and planted a vineyard. He drank of the wine and became drunk, and uncovered himself inside his tent. Ham, the father of Canaan, saw the nakedness of his father, and told his two brothers outside. (9:20–22)

The phrase "uncovered himself" indicates that Noah found himself in an inappropriate sexual situation. On top of that, he was drunk. How could such a righteous man get drunk in his tent and blatantly uncover himself? Noah had a depraved nature that led him to sin against the Lord.

Moses

We consider Moses to be one of the greatest saints in all of Scripture. God used him mightily to lead the Hebrew people out of slavery in Egypt. God chose him to receive the Law and unveil it to the Hebrews and to lead the Israelites through the wilderness on their way to the Promised Land. But Moses had a dark side, too. When he was about forty years old, he angrily murdered an Egyptian in an attempt to enact his own plan of deliverance for the Hebrews (Exodus 2:1–12; Acts 7:25–28). Forty years later, he resisted God's call to be His spokesman to Pharaoh and the Hebrews (Exodus 3:1–4:17). Moreover, during an outbreak of complaints among the Hebrews, Moses chose to disregard God's way of handling the problem and instead responded in a fit of rage (Numbers 20:2–12). Due to Moses's outburst of anger, God refused to allow him to enter the Promised Land. Clearly, Moses was also depraved.

David

Many years after the Hebrews entered the Promised Land, God chose a young shepherd named David to reign as king over His people (Psalm 78:70–71). The Bible calls David "a man after God's own heart" (1 Samuel 13:14; compare to Acts 13:22). In fact, for the first time in Israel's history, the nation rose to economic, military, and spiritual prominence under David's rule. But, great as David was, he still had a sinful nature. One fateful evening, he took a walk on his palace roof and saw a beautiful woman bathing (2 Samuel 11:2). With a body and heart brimming with lust, he sent for her and "lay with her" (11:3–4). Bathsheba conceived that night, and because David was desperate to cover his tracks, he engineered the death of Uriah, Bathsheba's husband. Bathsheba became David's wife. Adultery, deceit, and murder—all sinful acts committed by a believer. Why? David was depraved, pure and simple.

Peter

Turning to the New Testament, we encounter a hard-working fisherman named Peter, who gave up his trade to follow Christ. In one of his greatest moments, he identified Jesus as "the Christ, the Son of the Living God" (Matthew 16:16). But at Jesus's most difficult hour, Peter deserted Him and even denied Him (Matthew 26:47–56, 69–74). Another faithful follower fell prey to the corruption within.

Paul

The apostle Paul ranks as the best-known evangelist, church planter, writer, and theologian of the early church. Yet he openly admitted his struggle with sin, writing:

> For what I am doing, I do not understand; for I am not practic-
> ing what I would like to do, but I am doing the very thing I
> hate. But if I do the very thing I do not want to do, I agree with
> the Law, confessing that the Law is good. So now, no longer am
> I the one doing it, but sin which dwells in me. For I know that
> nothing good dwells in me, that is, in my flesh, for the willing
> is present in me, but the doing of the good is not. For the good
> that I want, I do not do, but I practice the very evil that I do
> not want. (Romans 7:15–19)

Like Paul, we may sincerely desire to please God, but even our best wishes and intentions are often thwarted by the depravity that lurks within our hearts and minds.

Do these five biblical portraits make you feel disappointed or encouraged in your spiritual walk? Why?

_____

_____

_____

_____

ONE GREAT EXCEPTION

Although these vignettes have painted a bleak picture of humanity, all is not lost. One Man, the God-Man, broke the horrible, destructive cycle of depravity. Jesus Christ, the Son of God, took on a perfect human nature and lived His life in complete obedience to the Father. Then He, who never committed a single sin, paid the penalty for *our* sin by dying on the cross in our place. By trusting in Him as our Savior, we will receive forgiveness and the power to overcome sin (Romans 7:24–8:39). That's fantastic news!

In Case You Were Wondering

Q: I'm confused about the "sin nature" that I often hear other Christians talking about. After I became a Christian, did I lose my sin nature? If not, then what separates me as a believer from non-Christians?

A: The marvelous working of God in the life of a believer begins at the point of faith in Christ. The Bible speaks of a believer's life before Christ as the "old man," while the "new man" represents a Christian's spiritual rebirth. However, the apostle Paul's teaching that the "old man was crucified" with Christ (Romans 6:6 NKJV) and yet still exists as something that we as believers must choose to "lay aside" (Ephesians 4:22) has led to some misunderstanding about what we call our "old nature" and our "new nature."

This confusion stems, in part, from a vague understanding of the term "nature." The expression never refers specifically to a person or thing but to the *qualities* or *characteristics* of a person or thing. For example, Jesus has two natures—human and divine—eternally joined in one person. While He lived on earth, Christ expressed both His humanity and divinity as a single man. His dual natures existed in perfect harmony. Our "sinful nature" and our "saintly nature," on the other hand, do not.

From one perspective, we have two natures because the attributes of both sin and righteousness remain within us, and these two natures are at war with one another (Romans 7:15–25). But from another perspective, God sees us with all "old things passed away" (2 Corinthians 5:17)—as people who now have righteous standing through the death and resurrection of Christ. Because Scripture teaches aspects of both perspectives, we cannot make them mutually exclusive.

Christ has "done away with" (or literally, "made powerless") our sinful nature (Romans 6:6). This doesn't mean the sinful nature no longer exists, but *it no longer has the power to make us sin.* The fact that Christians now find their identity in Christ alone does not mean the old, sinful nature no longer exerts its influence on us. It only means we don't have to respond to it because we have the power of the Holy Spirit to help us overcome the temptation to sin.

Two Available Options

When we boil down all that we've learned, we are faced with two options. *We can choose to live either as victims of our depravity or as victors through Jesus Christ's power.* We don't have to give in to our evil inclinations (Romans 6:12–19; James 1:12–18), but we cannot fight them successfully on our own. Only in Christ can we live victoriously. Which option will you choose?

SALVATION

13

"Mr. Smith, Meet Your Substitute"

Romans 3

When Peter Marshall preached, people listened. The main floor and balconies of his speaking venues were always packed with people, and those who could not find a seat stood to listen as he spoke the truth of the living God in clear, dramatic terms. Listen to a part of one of his sermons:

> Our country is full of Joneses, and they all have problems of one kind or another.
>
> Let's put the questions bluntly, as bluntly as Mr. Jones would put it.
>
> Can you and I really have communion with Christ as we would with earthly friends?
>
> Can we know personally the same Jesus whose words are recorded in the New Testament, Who walked the dusty trails of Galilee two thousand years ago?
>
> I don't mean can we treasure His words or try to follow His example or imagine Him.
>
> I mean, is He really alive? Can we actually meet Him, commune with Him, ask His help for our everyday affairs?
>
> The Gospel writers say "yes." A host of men and women down the ages say "yes." And the church says "yes."[1]

Appropriately, he entitled that sermon "Mr. Jones, Meet the Master." We've chosen a similar title for this chapter: "Mr. Smith, Meet Your Substitute." So, Mr. or Ms. Smith, this is for you. We're talking to everyone who happens to find themselves in this human predicament called "sin." Sin is the reason we need a substitute.

FOUR MAJOR ISSUES REGARDING SIN

Did you know that the third chapter of Romans contains your biography? The story may not be very attractive, but it's true. And so, Mr. or Ms. Smith, this is your life.

Our Condition: Totally Depraved

Read Romans 3:9–12. How does Paul characterize all of humanity in these verses?

_____

_____

_____

_____

Now, read verses 13 through 18. What descriptive terms does Paul use to illustrate our sin?

_____

_____

_____

Now, read Romans 3:19–26. To whom does the Law speak? Why?

_____

_____

_____

_____

According to verse 20, can anyone be justified by the works of the Law? What kind of knowledge comes through the Law?

_____

_____

_____

_____

Even when we try to hide our sin, our depraved human nature surfaces. Often, this happens when we least expect it and when we most want to keep our sin hidden.

God's Character: Infinitely Holy

God reigns in righteousness, perfection, and infinite holiness. His character and His Word are the "measuring rod," the moral standard against which all of us are compared and found lacking. The New Testament often refers to God's perfect standard as His "glory." We could paraphrase Romans 3:23 like this:

> For all have sinned [that's our condition] and fall short of the glory [that's His standard] of God.

God exists in the realm of absolute perfection, and His nature requires the same from us. God won't wink at our sin, shrug, and say, "Oh, that's okay. Don't worry about it!" His perfection requires our perfection, and that's the problem! Scripture tells us clearly that we've sinned and fallen short of the perfection of God.

But, you might say, "I'm a good person. I love others, and I try to do the right things. Don't my good works count for anything?" At times, we may be impressed by our own goodness, sincerity, sacrificial spirit, and altruism. But perfect? Never. Infinitely holy? No way. How about pure? Not even close. If you've ever had a selfish thought or said a word that hurt someone, you're not perfect. If you've ever said or done anything that contradicted God's commandments or principles, you're not perfect. Only God qualifies.

There's no way, Mr. or Ms. Smith, that we can match God's righteousness in our own strength or on our own merit.

Our Need: A Substitute

Scripture says, "God is Light, and in Him there is no darkness at all" (1 John 1:5). If we hope to know God and walk with Him, we must be as holy as He is. But we're lost in the darkness of sin. We need someone to do for us what we cannot do for ourselves—release us from the chains of sin. We need someone to be our substitute, so God provided the Savior.

God's Provision: A Savior

Romans 3 describes how God provided a way for us to be forgiven of our sin and reconciled to His perfection:

> [We] are justified freely by his grace through the redemption that came by Christ Jesus. God presented him as a sacrifice of atonement, through faith in his blood. He did this to demonstrate his justice, because in his forbearance he had left the sins committed beforehand unpunished—he did it to demonstrate his justice at the present time, so as to be just and the one who justifies those who have faith in Jesus. (Romans 3:24–26 NIV)

Take your pen and underline the words having to do with God's justice in the above verses. How many times do these terms appear?

_____

_____

_____

_____

Why do you think Paul placed so much emphasis on justice?

_____

_____

_____

_____

You've just been introduced to your righteous substitute. He's Christ, the sinless and perfect Son of God. His death for you was effective because He was the only One who could qualify as your substitute before God. Sin requires a penalty—death—in order for God's righteous demands to be satisfied. That's why the cross is so significant! It became the place where God laid our sin upon Jesus so that we wouldn't have to bear it anymore. There on the cross, Christ paid the price for our sin in full.

Have you ever stopped to think about the staggering cost of your salvation? Name some of the sacrifices, trials, and painful events that Christ suffered while on earth.

_____

_____

_____

_____

Now, write several sentences thanking Him for enduring the cross on your behalf.

_____

_____

_____

_____

Getting to the Root

In Romans 3:24, the word *justified* appears. This word, translated from the Greek legal term *dikaioō*, means "to show to be righteous; to declare righteous."[2] Justification is a merciful act of God by which He declares us righteous when we believe in Him, even though we're in a sinful state. He sees us wallowing around in the swamp of our sinfulness, and He reaches down and rescues us. When we believe in Jesus Christ, trusting Him completely by faith, He cleanses us from our sin. We can picture God proclaiming, "Declared righteous! Forgiven! Pardoned!"

Pardon from God and Christ's righteousness come to us only when we trust Jesus as our Lord and Savior. The only way we can approach Him in our lost condition is by faith. When we do this, God welcomes us into His intimate favor. Clothed in Christ's righteousness, we can enjoy God's fellowship. At that epochal moment, He declares us righteous before Him. All of this is included in what it means to be *justified*.

We could think of the cross as a sponge—a "spiritual sponge" that has absorbed all the past, present, and future sins of mankind. In one excruciating moment, Christ bore the crushing weight of all of our sins and iniquities, satisfying the righteous demands of the Father and reconciling our debt. He set us free from sin's power over us once and for all. He also granted us total redemption (Romans 3:24). We were given liberty, so we never have to return to the slave market of sin. And remember, the rescue occurred because of what *Christ* did—not because of anything that *we* did!

 ## In Case You Were Wondering

Q: Is it possible to do something that would cause me to lose my salvation?

A: Romans 8:38–39 says that no "created thing" can separate us from the love of God, given to us through Jesus Christ. Since you and I are "created thing[s]," Paul states very strongly that under no circumstance could we ever do something that would cause us to lose our salvation.

Earlier in the same chapter of Romans, Paul says that "those whom [God] justified, He also glorified" (8:30). From our perspective, we have not yet been glorified; that will not happen in this life. But from God's perspective, it's already done. Our salvation is complete in His sight (including the initial moment of salvation called *justification*, the ongoing work of salvation called *sanctification*, and the final work of salvation called *glorification*). What greater assurance do we need that God would not under any circumstance undo the work which He has already completed? Jesus affirmed this truth in John 10:27–28: "My sheep hear My voice, and I know them, and they follow Me; and I give eternal life to them, and they will never perish; and no one will snatch them out of My hand."

A seasoned Bible teacher once said, "Man is incurably addicted to trying to earn his own salvation." Have you seen this idea manifested in your own life or in the lives of others? If so, how?

_____

_____

_____

_____

Not only is earning our own salvation impossible, it's also a waste of our precious time, energy, and resources. Scripture teaches that salvation is a "by-faith, not-by-works" transaction. Romans 4:4–5 makes this fact clear:

> Now to the one who works, his wage is not credited as a favor, but as what is due. But to the one who does not work, but believes in Him who justifies the ungodly, *his faith is credited as righteousness,* . . . (emphasis added)

Just think of your paycheck, Mr. or Ms. Smith. When your employer gives you your paycheck at the end of each pay period, you don't drop to your knees in gratitude and say, "Oh, thank you so much for this generous gift!" You probably take the check and don't give much thought to saying thanks. Why? Because you've *earned* that money. You know full well that there's an enormous difference between an earned wage and a free gift!

God says that salvation is for "the one who does *not* work, but believes . . ." (John 6:29; Romans 4:5). Let me spell it out for you by way of review:

Our Condition:	Totally Depraved
God's Character:	Infinitely Holy
Our Need:	A Substitute
God's Provision:	A Savior

When God provided our Substitute, the Savior, He said to each one of us, "Here's my gift to you." In 2 Corinthians 5:20–21, we find these words:

> Therefore, we are ambassadors for Christ, as though God were making an appeal though us; we beg you on behalf of Christ, be reconciled to God. He made Him who knew no sin to be sin on our behalf, so that we might become the righteousness of God in Him.

Pay close attention to the pronouns.

> He [God, the Father] made Him [God, the Son] who knew no
> sin to be sin on our behalf [that happened at the cross], so that
> we [the sinners] might become the righteousness of God in
> Him [Christ].

The cross. There's no other way! But how can the sinner in the black hole of his need ever know God in the spotless white of all His righteousness? Second Corinthians 5:21 tells us: by coming to know Him who knew no sin—the One who became sin on our behalf. Put your pride in your pocket, Mr. or Ms. Smith. You need a substitute. You need a defense attorney—an eternal advocate. And in Christ and Christ alone, you have one.

Digging Deeper

Three Crucial Questions

Three questions are crucial to our understanding of our salvation:

Question	Answer
1. Is there any hope for lost sinners?	Yes; Christ!
2. Isn't there any work a sinner can do to earn God's favor?	No; believe!
3. Is there any way for the saved to lose the gift?	No, never!

First question: Is there any hope for lost sinners? Yes; Christ! He died for our sins and was placed in the grave as proof of His death. He rose from the dead bodily, miraculously, in proof of our justification (Romans 4:25). If you believe that He died and rose for you, you have eternal life. It's a gift.

Second question: Isn't there any work a sinner can do to earn God's favor? Don't I have to add to it? No; just believe! Trying to add to God's work is like trying to pay back friends who have hosted a sumptuous dinner for you at their home. Trying to pay for the gift cheapens it and robs your friends of the joy of giving. But today, men and women all around the world are reaching in their pockets and asking, "Okay, God, how much do I owe You?"

Third Question: Is there any way to lose the gift? No, never! If you have to work to earn something, then it follows that if you STOP working, you could lose it. And that would mean it wasn't a gift; it was simply something that you earned. Don't try to turn God's gift into a wage! If salvation could be earned, no one would be able to determine how much work would be enough to earn it—or how little work would cause one to lose it. Salvation is a *gift*.

Two Possible Responses

We're back to the basics, Mr. or Ms. Smith. You can either believe and accept God's gift of salvation or you can reject it. And you can go right on living, by the way. God won't suddenly send a thunderbolt down from heaven to end your life just because you refused to accept His gift. That's not the way He operates! He holds out His grace, and He makes it available even if we choose to reject it. But eternal life can be yours only through the salvation that God offers by means of the birth, death, and resurrection of His own Son, Jesus Christ.

One Final Reminder

Unfortunately, sin is a terminal disease, and you've got it! Sin leads to physical death for each and every one of us. You may believe that you still have plenty of time on this earth, but all you know for sure is that you have RIGHT NOW. Are you hearing the still, small voice of God within you, asking you to confess your sin and commit your life to Him?

Remember our introductory story about Peter Marshall? This great preacher once asked his congregation:

> . . . if you were walking down the street, and someone came up behind you and tapped you on the shoulder . . . what would you do? Naturally, you would turn around. Well, that is exactly

what happens in the spiritual world. A man walks on through life—with the external call ringing in his ears, but with no response stirring in his heart, and then suddenly, without any warning, the Spirit taps him on the shoulder. The tap on the shoulder is the almighty power of God acting without help or hindrance . . . so as to produce a new creature, and to lead him in to the particular work which God has for him.[3]

Are you feeling a tap on your shoulder? If so, respond to God's leading. Tell the Lord you have felt His tap, and you want to take the opportunity to confess your sin and accept His gift of eternal life. Thank Him for giving you His Son, Jesus Christ. (If you'd like more guidance and direction in this process, please turn to the "How to Begin a Relationship with God" section in the back of this workbook.)

If you've taken this step of faith today, Mr. or Ms. Smith, congratulations! You've just met your Substitute.

14

THE REMEDY FOR OUR DISEASE

Selected Scriptures

Many centuries ago, Portuguese settlers spent ten years building a magnificent cathedral on a high hill overlooking the harbor of Macao. Many thought the structure would stand forever, but one day, a typhoon's fierce winds leveled the entire building except for the front wall of the cathedral. Today, that lone wall rises against a deep blue background of ocean melting into sky. And against that wall stands an enormous bronze cross, challenging the elements, declaring to the wind and the waves, "You may tear down this cathedral, but you'll never destroy the cross!"

In 1825, Sir John Bowring was struggling in a terrible storm in that same harbor off the South China coast. His ship had been battered to pieces, and he had no idea where to find land. Hanging on to the wreckage of his ship in the tumultuous sea, sure that he was about to die, he suddenly caught a glimpse of that huge old bronze cross positioned atop the cathedral wall. This beacon of hope showed Bowring which direction to go. His ensuing rescue was so dramatic that he wrote a poem expressing his gratitude to God for saving his life. This poem was later put to music, and for over a hundred and fifty years, God's people have sung Bowring's message:

> In the cross of Christ I glory,
> Towering o'er the wrecks of time;
> All the light of sacred story
> Gathers round its head sublime.
>
> When the sun of bliss is beaming
> Light and love upon my way,
> From the cross the radiance streaming
> Adds more luster to the day.[1]

Just as the sight of the cross gave Bowring hope of rescue, the cross of Christ has led to our rescue from sin. But we need to understand that it isn't the cross itself that we honor. Some Christians place too much emphasis on the cross on which Jesus died. We place large crosses inside our churches and wear small crosses around our necks. We talk about the cross and sing songs about the cross. But usually, we take the gruesomeness and gore of the cross away and replace it with beautiful, smooth crosses made of expensive materials.

We give honor to the cross as a symbol of Christ's death in our place, and we lift up the message of the cross. But we aren't supposed to exalt the literal cross. Not the original cross beams; those rugged, blood-soaked pieces of timber that stood on Golgotha centuries ago. Not the actual wood and nails. Not the shape or location of the cross. The One who hung upon it is the One whom we honor. We appreciate what the cross represents, because it is there that Christ paid the price for our sins in full, but we don't worship the cross itself.

Once it has served its purpose, the physical cross *itself* loses significance. But the Savior who died upon that cross lives on. And the redemption He provided continues to be significant and effective. When we sing about the cross or when we speak of holding high the cross, we're honoring what it *represents*—the day when Christ purchased our spiritual freedom. Our Substitute died in our place, providing the remedy for our spiritual disease.

A Prediction of the Substitute

The Old Testament contains a number of detailed predictions concerning Jesus's death on the cross. We find one in Isaiah 53, which emphasizes the attributes of Christ as the suffering Messiah and explains the completed, saving work He accomplished at Calvary.

Jesus's Suffering

Read Isaiah 53:1–2. What do these verses say about Jesus's appearance?

_____

_____

_____

_____

Nothing about Jesus's appearance was particularly attractive. He didn't stand out from anyone else living in His day. He looked like any other adult Jew. There was no visible aura around Him or halo above His head. When He walked down a dirt road, He got dirty like everyone else. When He was tired, He slept like everyone else. He felt hunger and thirst. He experienced pain and sorrow. He possessed the marks of humanity just like everyone else. So, how was He different? He was perfect on the inside. He was not only man, He was God. But you couldn't tell it just by looking at Him.

Read Isaiah 53:3. What descriptions of Jesus's pain and sorrow does Isaiah provide in this verse? List them below.

_____

_____

_____

_____

What term does Isaiah repeat in lines 1 and 4 of verse 3?

_____

Getting to the Root

The Hebrew term *bazah*, translated "despised" in Isaiah 53:3, means "treated with carelessness or contempt; despicable; disdained." [2]

How does this definition add to your understanding of how Jesus was treated?

_____

_____

_____

_____

> **What images do this passage and this definition evoke in your mind?**
>
> _____
>
> _____
>
> _____
>
> _____

Jesus's Solution to Our Dilemma

Jesus's solution to our sin dilemma wasn't easy. In fact, it was one of the most painful, excruciating experiences that any person has ever encountered.

Let's examine the work Jesus did in order to offer us salvation. Read Isaiah 53:4–6. What burdens did Jesus bear on the cross? List them here.

_____

_____

_____

_____

Notice that He bore *our* griefs and *our* sorrows, not His own. Part of the burden of the cross was that Jesus took the penalty for our sin and carried it to the very end. That explains our need for Him as our Substitute.

But how did people respond to Him? They gave Him no respect! Their own sin and depravity blinded them. They did not recognize or value His worth as the Bearer of their sins.

Read 1 Peter 2:21–25. According to these verses, what attacks were made against Christ?

_____

_____

_____

_____

What was His response?

_____

_____

_____

_____

According to verse 24, why did He bear our sins? By what have we been healed?

_____

_____

_____

_____

How are we characterized in verse 25? How is Jesus described? What does this image of Jesus mean to you personally?

_____

_____

_____

_____

Why did Jesus, the perfect Lamb of God, choose to experience so much pain? We find the answer in Isaiah 53:6:

> All of us like sheep have gone astray,
> Each of us has turned to His own way;
> But the Lord has caused the iniquity of us all
> To fall on Him.

The physical agony of the cross defies description, but the spiritual suffering that Christ endured was even worse. We can't even imagine the horror of the separation that occurred between the Father and His Son. For the first and only time in all of eternity, the Father and the Son were separated as Jesus "became" sin on our behalf. This severance caused the Lord Jesus to scream, "*Eli, Eli, lama sabachthani* . . . My God, My God, why have You forsaken Me?" (Matthew 27:46). At that moment, Jesus bore the crushing weight of all mankind's iniquity.

AN EXPLANATION OF THE SACRIFICE

To understand the reason for Jesus's sacrificial death, we must go to the handbook of Law and worship that the Jews used for centuries—the book of Leviticus. Let's look at four stages that occurred when a person came to offer a sacrifice to God.

In the ancient world, when people found themselves in sin and broken fellowship with God, it was essential that they offer an animal sacrifice. The sacrifice could be a sheep or a goat, a bull, a heifer, turtledoves, or pigeons, depending on the occasion. The details of such sacrifices are spelled out in this ancient book of worship used by the Jews and their Levitical priests.

The process is described in four stages. *In the first stage, the sinner brought an animal to the altar.*

Read Leviticus 4:1–3. In this passage, what type of animal was the sinner commanded to offer?

_____

_____

As soon as a person realized that sin had come into his or her life, whether intentional or unintentional, he or she knew that the sin had caused a breach in his or her fellowship with God. To heal the breach, he or she had to bring an animal to the altar to be sacrificed by the priest. Not just any animal, but one without defect. The animal would become a "sin offering," which provided purification for unintentional sins.

During the second stage, the sinner laid his hand on the animal.

Read Leviticus 4:4. What specific actions was the sinner to take with regard to the sacrificial animal? Why do you think God required these steps?

_____

_____

_____

_____

The sinner laid his or her hand upon the head of the animal. This act symbolized the transfer of guilt from himself or herself to the animal, making the sacrifice a substitute for the sinner.

In the third stage, the animal was sacrificed.

Read Leviticus 5:6–10. What types of animals were required for the guilt offering, according to verse 6? (The guilt offering was a type of sin offering.)

_____

_____

According to verse 7, if a person could not afford these, what was he or she to bring for a sin offering and a burnt offering? (A burnt offering was another type of offering for sin.)

_____

_____

If a person brought the latter offerings, what was each one for? How was the priest commanded to sacrifice each one for a sin offering?

_____

_____

_____

_____

Have you ever read anything like that in your life? Just "nip" the front of its neck so there is a sprinkling of the blood. Scripture defines every detail clearly. Why is there so much emphasis on the shedding of the blood? Look at this key verse in the book of Leviticus:

> For the life of the flesh is in the blood, and I have given it to
> you on the altar to make atonement for your souls; for it is the
> blood by reason of the life that makes atonement. (17:11)

Look at the word "atonement." It's mentioned twice in this single verse. God devised this plan: by the shedding of blood, the sin which separated us from God would be covered. The blood of the animal would bring reconciliation between sinful humanity and our holy God. The Hebrew term is _kaphar_, which means "to cover over, pacify, make propitiation, or appease." [3] The blood would satisfy God's righteous demand of death for sin.

In the fourth stage, the blood was poured out or sprinkled as God required.

Read Leviticus 4:9. In what places was the anointed priest commanded to put the blood?

_____

_____

_____

_____

Since the times of Cain and Abel, God's people have placed enormous emphasis on blood sacrifices. Lambs were slain by the thousands at Passover. Priests offered blood sacrifices day in and day out. _God required it._ That's why we must resist the modern tendency to remove the references to blood and its significance from our theology, our Bibles, and our music. Without the blood of Jesus Christ shed on the cross for us, there is no forgiveness of sin. Period.

Digging Deeper

It Is Finished!

Can you imagine living thousands of years ago and having to slit the throats of live animals and drain their blood, day after wearisome day? The repetition, the mess, the noise, and the stench would have been absolutely overwhelming. And, to make things worse, animal sacrifices never permanently removed sin. The people received only momentary relief and temporary forgiveness from their guilt. Their sins were "covered," but not entirely removed. People would go on their way rejoicing, and their sense of forgiveness would last for a while, but they'd soon fall back into sin and return with another animal for sacrifice, and the entire gruesome cycle would start again.

But when Jesus died on the cross and poured out His blood as a sacrifice for our transgressions, He cried out *"Tetelestai!"* which means "It is finished!" (John 19:30). This Greek word is based on the legal term *teleo*, meaning "to bring to an end, complete, fulfill, accomplish, carry out, finish, carry out, pay, or perfect."[4] The sacrifice of the Lamb of God was carried out once for all. His death on the cross finished the task and paid our debt.

In your life, what does it mean to live with the knowledge that your sin debt has already been paid in full?

_____

_____

_____

_____

In Case You Were Wondering

Q: Why did God require a seemingly cruel practice like animal sacrifices? If these sacrifices were so important in Old Testament times, why don't we offer them today?

A: The stench of death that rises from the pages of Leviticus quickly creates a conflict in our perception of God. Is this God who required blood sacrifice after blood sacrifice the same God who wants us to call Him Father, the same God who tenderly shepherds us and showers His blessings on us?

People in ancient cultures believed that pagan gods required blood on the altar in order to appease their appetites and as bribes to keep them from cursing those under their dominion. Our God, however, is neither a carnivore to be fed nor a bully to be bribed—He hates violence and death even more than we do! But He is perfectly righteous, as He declared in Leviticus 10:3: "By those who come near Me I will be treated as holy, and before all the people I will be honored." God desired a relationship with the Israelites, but His holiness prevented sin from entering into His presence. Because all of the Israelites were sinners, the blood spilled on the altar served as a *covering*; it hid the sins of the people from God's face so that they could remain in relationship with Him.

As beneficial as this system was for the reconciliation of the Israelites to God, a temporary sacrifice could provide only a temporary solution. A lamb without physical blemish covered sin for a moment; only a Lamb without *spiritual* blemish could wash away sin for eternity. Christ's blood shed for us did not merely cover our sin for a while; it removed our sin *forever*. His sacrifice allows us to come into God's presence again and again because our sins are not simply covered or hidden; they are completely forgiven and removed from us "as far as the east is from the west" (Psalm 103:12).

THE SUFFICIENCY OF CHRIST'S SACRIFICE

Let's explore the sufficiency of Christ's sacrifice. Read Hebrews 10:1–4. Can the Law or the blood sacrifices of animals make us perfect? If they *were* able to make us perfect, what would we lose?

_____

_____

_____

_____

According to verse 3, what was one of the purposes of the animal sacrifices?

_____

_____

_____

_____

Read Hebrews 10:10–12. After offering up His body for all of mankind, what did Jesus do? What does this action represent?

_____

_____

_____

_____

Christ never again has to die! After Jesus's once-for-all sacrificial death, the Father said, "I am satisfied." The payment made on the cross satisfied the Father's demands against sin. How do we know He's satisfied? He raised His Son from the grave and seated Him at His right hand in glory. The transaction made on the cross paid for all of our sins and all of the Father's wrath. If God is satisfied with the death of His Son, and we find our identity and salvation in His Son, then God the Father is satisfied with us!

Thankfully, we don't have to live under the demanding slavery of working, begging, pleading, fearing, bargaining, or paying penance to find favor with God. Once we've placed our faith and trust in Christ, we're just as safe and secure in our salvation as the Son is before His Father.

A DECLARATION OF THE SAVIOR

The declaration of the Savior is found in the final verse of 2 Corinthians 5, which we read in the previous chapter.

> He made Him who knew no sin to be sin on our behalf, so that we might become the righteousness of God in Him. (5:21)

Remember the laying of hands on the sacrificial animal? We can think of Christ's death as the time when He allowed all of mankind to place our sinful hands on Him and say, "All of our sins are now transferred to You. At this moment, you willingly bear those sins in our place." Christ, the spotless Lamb, took all of our sins and guilt upon Himself at the cross. His work of salvation is a completed work. God has provided full redemption of sin for all of us when we choose to accept Christ. Jesus has already paid the penalty for our sins—past, present, and future.

Sir John Bowring looked toward the South China coast and saw the magnificent sight of the cross offering its eternal, triumphant message of hope and deliverance. And, thanks to the extraordinary sacrifice Christ made for us, we can do the same.

The Return of Christ

15

His Coming Is Sure . . . Are You?

Selected Scriptures

We've all probably seen the bumper sticker that reads, "In case of rapture, this car will be unmanned." Over time, people have developed several tongue-in-cheek versions of this bumper sticker, including, "In case of rapture, this car will swerve as my mother-in-law takes the wheel!" and "In case of rapture, can I have your car?"

People have a wide variety of views and interpretations regarding the end times, especially relating to what the Bible says about Jesus's return. In order to approach the subject with truth, balance, and a godly perspective, we must first seek to understand what Scripture teaches about end-time events and then determine how we can best apply this truth.

Extremes That Prevent Balance

Fanaticism

Some Christians seem to let go of their common sense when discussing the end times. Their zeal and fanaticism for discussing these events invariably drives others away. They tend to overreact to teachings of prophecy and then try to force their own interpretations on others. They may read end-time prophecy into almost every news story or natural disaster. They may spend more time focusing on the future than on the present. They may lead irresponsible lives, spending their time and money carelessly. After all, their imminent departure from planet Earth will provide the perfect escape from responsibility! The ultimate extremists are those who set specific dates, then quit their jobs and mooch from others as they wait for the Lord's return. Shirking our responsibilities by using Christ's coming as an excuse isn't just poor stewardship; it's abominable theology. Not once does Scripture condone personal irresponsibility on the basis of one's confidence in Christ's return. Biblical, faithful anticipation of His return is one thing; reckless fanaticism is quite another.

Theological Ignorance

Theological ignorance represents another extreme. "Personal indifference" might be another way to describe this attitude. The indifferent individual sees no reason to be on the alert for Christ's return. In fact, this person may doubt seriously that the rapture will ever occur. Most Christians who fall into this category express little or no interest in their responsibility for evangelism because they feel no sense of urgency for reaching the lost before Christ returns. But God desires for Christians to live the Christian life passionately, sharing the gospel with every person.

The average human lifespan is less than eighty years, and that's not long at all! The anticipation of Christ's return should stoke the fire of evangelism in our hearts and keep us involved in God's work. He planned it that way!

Needed Balance

We can achieve balance by remaining patient, informed, and aware, realizing that Christ's return could occur at any moment. We're called to live our lives as responsibly as we can.

Let's look at 2 Peter. The apostle writes authoritatively as an eyewitness of the Lord Jesus Christ. Read 2 Peter 1:16–19. What did Peter and the disciples choose not to follow? What did they personally witness?

_____

_____

_____

_____

What did God the Father say about Christ?

_____

_____

_____

_____

Now, read 2 Peter 3:3–4. Whom did Peter say would come in the last days? What would these people say?

_____

_____

_____

_____

Read verses 5 and 6. What past event escapes the notice of these individuals?

_____

_____

_____

_____

Next, Peter moves from discussing past events to describing the future. Indeed, the very fact of a past global judgment proves that God has the ability to do it again. Read verses 7–9. According to verse 7, how will the heavens and earth be destroyed in the future?

_____

_____

_____

Why does God appear to be "slow" in keeping His promise of sending Christ back to earth? See 3:9.

_____

_____

_____

_____

 What does this mean for you in regard to your own life and relationships? See 3:11–15.

_____

_____

_____

_____

Jesus is going to return—at the time of the rapture for His church and at the Second Coming to reign over the earth—so let's get ready! We shouldn't mistake our Lord's current patience for apathy, powerlessness, or permanent absence. Jesus *is* coming back.

Digging Deeper

Scriptural Support for Christ's Return

Before looking at other Scripture verses, let's embark on a brief safari. These facts from biblical prophecy about Christ's return may surprise you:

- One out of every 30 verses in the Bible mentions the subject of Christ's return or the end of time.

- 23 of the 27 New Testament books mention Christ's return.

- Job, Moses, David, Isaiah, Jeremiah, Daniel, and most of the minor prophets mention Christ's return in their writings.

- Christ often spoke specifically about His own return to earth.

- Throughout the centuries, Christ's disciples and followers adamantly believed, wrote, and taught that Christ would someday return to earth.

Obviously, the return of Christ is an extremely significant issue. Yet Christians throughout the generations have experienced confusion regarding this doctrine and the order of future events.

In Case You Were Wondering

Q: I'm confused about the order in which the rapture of the church, the Second Coming, and the judgments will occur. Can you help?

A: This simple chart illustrates the order in which end-time events will occur, according to Scripture. The corresponding Bible passages are included for further reference. The passage from 1 Thessalonians lists the order of the events that will occur during the rapture. The other passages listed give the order of end-time events for the Tribulation through the establishment of the new heaven and the new earth.

Chart of the End Times[1]

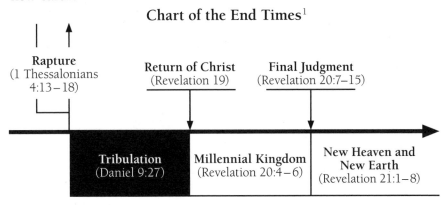

SCRIPTURES THAT DESCRIBE OUR DESTINY

One dark night in a second-story room in Jerusalem, Jesus ate His "last supper" with His disciples. There, He revealed the startling truth that His death was only hours away. The eleven must have wanted to stop their ears from hearing Him say, "I'm going to leave you. I'm going back to My Father."

Read John 14:1–2. What impacts you the most about these words that Jesus spoke? What evidence do we have of heaven as a real place?

_____

_____

_____

_____

Heaven, our eternal destiny, is real. It isn't a figment of our imagination or a state of mind; it's a reality. Heaven is a literal place that Jesus is preparing for His own. He says so in verse 3! He says, "I will come again and receive you to Myself." That's a direct promise from His lips. This is also the first mention of the rapture these disciples had ever heard.

This kind of teaching must have stunned the disciples. They had anticipated the immediate establishment of Jesus's earthly kingdom. They expected Jesus to rule as the King of kings and Lord of lords in Jerusalem before the end of their generation. They envisioned themselves as high-ranking rulers in His royal court. They thought, with great delight, that they would witness the overthrow of Rome, Israel's cruel oppressor. But Christ put all of that on hold and taught them that His present spiritual kingdom would be characterized by humility and love. Shortly thereafter, Jesus went to the cross. He died and was placed in a tomb. But three days later, He emerged in bodily form from the tomb, victorious over death.

Now, let's turn our attention to two more passages that are worth examining: 1 Corinthians 15:50–58 and 1 Thessalonians 4:13–18. Both of these Scripture passages describe our destiny as Christians. The 1 Corinthians passage emphasizes the *changes* that will occur in us when Christ returns. The 1 Thessalonians passage emphasizes the *order of events* that will occur in the future.

1 Corinthians

After developing a thorough statement on the resurrection, the apostle Paul presents a transition in 1 Corinthians 15:50:

> Now I say this, brethren, that flesh and blood cannot inherit the kingdom of God; nor does the perishable inherit the imperishable.

Paul is talking to us "earthlings," people who have been earthbound all our lives. We're all in the process of living—and dying. Remember your younger days, when you felt different and looked different? Now, we all bear physical signs that we're aging. We have loved ones in their seventies and eighties, maybe even their nineties, who certainly reveal the "perishable" nature and mortality of mankind. In order for these bodies of ours to last throughout eternity, *there must be a change* so that our bodies are made ageless. We must undergo some type of transformation that will prepare us for eternity. Our eternal existence will not be merely a spiritual existence, but a bodily existence as well. For this reason, in the next three verses, Paul emphasizes the future changes we will undergo. Take time to read 1 Corinthians 15:51–53.

Getting to the Root

In 1 Corinthians 15:51, Paul calls this revelation "a mystery." In our day, a *mystery* suggests something complex, like a riddle. But in Paul's day, the Greek word *mustērion* meant "a secret" or "a truth that few people know." One source lists the meaning as "a mystery or secret doctrine."[2] It's like Paul was writing, "Listen, I want to tell you a secret." What was Paul's secret? A generation will be alive at the time Christ comes, and those living believers will be instantly changed and taken to be with Him forever. Not only will the dead be raised and changed at the rapture, but those believers who are alive will also be changed.

Now, read 15:54–55. What will be "swallowed up"? In what will it be "swallowed up"?

_____

_____

According to verse 56, what is the sting of death?

_____

_____

In verse 57, what does God give us? Through whom does He give it?

_____

_____

What should we do as a result? See 15:58.

_____

_____

_____

_____

What reassurance do we have about the work we do here on earth?

_____

_____

_____

_____

1 Thessalonians

Take some time to read 1 Thessalonians 4:13–17. From this passage, we can make five major observations concerning our attitude and behavior in regard to the end times.

1. *We are to be informed.* The Lord doesn't approve of an attitude that says, "Well, actually, nobody can know for sure what is going to happen. Who knows if Jesus is coming back or not? We'll just go about our business and hope that things will work out in the end." God expects us to be informed and knowledgeable about His plan. Knowing what to expect in the future gives us confidence in the present.

2. *We are not to grieve as those without hope.* Death brings sorrow. Sorrow brings tears. Tears are part of the grieving process. God never tells us not to grieve; He simply says that we shouldn't grieve "as those who have no hope." Naturally, we should be free to express our deep grief when we lose someone precious to us. Yet even in our grief, we can maintain joy and hope in God's goodness and His plan for our lives. We have His promise of eternal life that transcends the grave.

3. *We are to face death without fear.* Christ's own resurrection is important to us because we can anticipate rising as He did. If He had not come back from the dead, we wouldn't have a right to expect to be raised. But no one will ever see a dead Jesus. Why? He has been raised. His tomb is empty. Because He lives, all fear is gone!

4. *We are to know the order of events with regard to the rapture.*

According to 4:16, what will happen first?

What three things will accompany the Lord's descent?

1. _____

2. _____

3. _____

According to the same verse, who will rise first?

_____

Who will rise next? Where will they meet the Lord? See 4:17.

_____

_____

5. We are to comfort one another with the knowledge that Jesus will come back for us. This knowledge is a comfort to us if we believe in Him. We have eternal life only by placing our faith in the One who has already conquered death, hell, and the grave.

But our hope also carries a responsibility. Forty days after His resurrection, Jesus stood on the Mount of Olives with His followers. While Christ was there, just before He ascended to heaven, the disciples again brought up the subject of His coming kingdom.

Read Acts 1:6–8. Judging from their question in verse 6, what did the disciples want Jesus to do? Why do you think they asked Him this question? What did they expect from Jesus?

_____

_____

_____

_____

Instead, what did Jesus promise them in verses 7 and 8? From what source would it come?

_____

_____

_____

_____

As a result of this promise, what would His followers become? Where would they go to spread the gospel?

_____

_____

_____

_____

Read verses 9 through 11. Where did Jesus go? How does this correspond with the way in which He will return to earth a second time?

_____

_____

_____

_____

What message did the angels give about how Christ would return to earth at His Second Coming?

_____

_____

_____

_____

GROWING DEEP IN THE CHRISTIAN LIFE

SOME PASSAGES THAT DESCRIBE CHRIST'S SECOND COMING

To better understand the details of Christ's Second Coming, let's look at several verses of Scripture that underscore this critical prophecy.

Matthew 24 is a great place to start. Read 24:42–44. Matthew makes a surprising comparison between Jesus and what type of person? How will Christ's Second Coming be similar to the way this type of person operates?

_____

_____

_____

Now turn to Mark 8. Read verses 35–38. When Christ comes to earth a second time, what will happen to the one who wants to save his life (i.e., to choose his own way instead of following Christ)?

_____

_____

_____

_____

What will happen to the one who loses his life for the sake of Christ and the gospel?

_____

_____

What will happen to the one who is ashamed of Christ (i.e., refuses to believe)?

_____

_____

ACTIONS THAT REVEAL OUR READINESS

We can reveal our readiness for Christ's return in three ways:

- *First*, we walk by faith, not by what we see.

- *Second*, we live in peace, not in panic, with regard to the future.

- *Third*, we rely on our hope in God's promise for our future.

One day, Jesus will come back for us. If you're spiritually ready to meet Him, the thought of His coming should be a comfort to you—bringing peace. If you're not ready, the idea of His coming probably causes you a great deal of fear and uncertainty. The secret of eternal life is being sure you know the One who has the power to defeat the grave. His coming is sure—are you?

16

Until He Returns . . . What?

Selected Scriptures

We all have the same amount of time to spend each day. God has allotted twenty-four hours to each one of us. But, because we're products of our fast-paced society, we tend to act as if God has shortchanged us when it comes to time. We often make comments like "There just aren't enough hours in the day!" or "I'm sorry; I just don't have time." With all of our modern conveniences and technological advances, we *should* have more leisure time than people in any other period in history. But the opposite is true.

With all of our daily activities and responsibilities, we tend to push the central doctrines of the Bible onto the back burner. But these truths are vital to our daily Christian walk. For example, consider the return of Christ. What we believe about this important doctrine affects the way we live our lives. And if there's one thing we can know for sure, it's that Jesus *will* come back to earth one day! The book of Matthew records these authoritative words from the mouth of Jesus:

> Heaven and earth will pass away, but My words will not pass away.
>
> But of that day and hour no one knows, not even the angels of heaven, nor the Son, but the Father alone. For the coming of the Son of Man will be just like the days of Noah. For as in those days before the flood they were eating and drinking, marrying and giving in marriage, until the day that Noah entered the ark, and they did not understand until the flood came and took them all away; so will the coming of the Son of Man be. . . .
>
> Therefore be on the alert, for you do not know which day your Lord is coming. (24:35–39, 42)

The doctrine of the second coming of Christ encompasses a number of significant prophetic elements: the rapture, the tribulation, the actual Second Coming, and the millennial kingdom. Jesus's point in Matthew 24 is clear: those believers who are alive during the tribulation period will not know the exact moment when He will come to reign on earth, but they will know that He *will* return. And His return will happen at a time when they least expect it. Just as Christ told those believers to be ready, so He has called us to have our hearts prepared for when He comes for us at the rapture. Let's find out what it means to be ready.

CHRIST'S EMPHASIS ON GODLY LIVING

Why did Jesus spend so much time focusing people's attention on His return? Was it to stir up their emotions? Was it to pique their curiosity about Him? Was it to strike fear in the hearts of his opponents? Was it to shock people or to create a sensation? Actually, none of the above are true! As we read through several Bible passages that explain the return of Christ, we'll notice a vital recurring element: *an emphasis on living godly lives* because we know that Jesus will return someday.

Getting to the Root

In the book of Ephesians, Paul wrote:

> Be careful how you walk, not as unwise men but as wise, making the most of your time, because the days are evil. (5:15–16)

The word translated as "making the most" here is translated as "redeeming" in the King James Version of the Bible. The Greek term, *exagorazō*, means, "to buy up; ransom; rescue from loss; make the most; redeem."[1] Paul also used this verb in Galatians 3:13 and 4:5 in connection with believers' redemption from the Law. Used in the middle voice as it is in Ephesians 5, the term carries the connotation "to buy back for oneself."

Paul calls us to be on the alert because the days in which we live are evil. Satan is called "the evil one," and the evil of our days is greatly magnified by Satan's activity as the ruler of this age (see John 12:31; 14:30; Ephesians 2:2; 6:12). Worldly people, material things, and secular philosophies introduce us to ideas and values that are destructive and contrary to the purposes of God. We're called to actively "redeem" our time on earth by protecting ourselves from evil influences, bearing spiritual fruit, and shedding light in the darkness at every opportunity.

FOUR COMMANDS TO HELP US PREPARE

While we wait in eager anticipation for Christ to return for us, let's keep in mind these four simple commands. They represent God's "marching orders" for us as we wait for Christ:

- Occupy
- Purify
- Watch
- Worship

Occupy

First, *we're called to occupy our time wisely while we're on earth.* Luke, the writer of the third gospel, recorded a parable that Jesus told to emphasize the importance of living a responsible and mature Christian life while we wait for His return.

Read Luke 19:11–27. How many servants did the nobleman originally call? How many minas did each receive?

The money each servant received was equivalent to about three months' wages. The nobleman charged each servant with the responsibility to put his money to work by wisely investing it. Interestingly, the nobleman called all ten servants back to account for what they had been given, but only three men's responses are recorded in verses 16–21.

How much did the first servant earn with the money he was given? The second servant? The third servant?

_____

_____

_____

_____

What justification did the third servant offer for hoarding his mina rather than investing it?

_____

_____

_____

_____

What happened to the third servant's mina?

_____

_____

_____

_____

What surprises you, if anything, about this parable? What does it tell you about the economy of God's kingdom and the expectation of Christ's return?

_____

_____

_____

_____

To further explain this parable, scholar Walter L. Liefeld wrote:

> In passage after passage, [Luke] deals with Jesus' teaching about the future in general, the present and future aspects of the kingdom, and the consummation of God's purposes in history. Obviously this parable teaches that Jesus predicted an interval of time between his ascension and return. . . .
>
> Jesus has gone to the heavenly seat of authority till the time for his return. In the meantime, though his qualifications for kingship are impeccable, he has been rejected by those who should serve him as his subjects.[2]

Clearly, the nobleman in the parable expected his subjects to "do business" with the money he had given them. In the same way, Jesus wants us to "do business" while we wait for His return. The Lord expects us to use our time, talents, and financial resources wisely. He's pleased with those who invest what they have in order to reap a greater future reward.

What does it mean for us to *occupy* our time wisely? We do so when we choose to live responsibly, work diligently, plan wisely, think realistically, and invest carefully. When we stop and think through the whole of Scripture from the Old Testament to the New, we find that God never approves of laziness. The book of Proverbs offers ample proof of this truth! God expects us to exercise spiritual passion, wisdom, discipline, and diligence. He desires us to live a joyful, well-ordered life that offers a powerful testimony to others.

Read 2 Thessalonians 3:6–9. What command did Paul give?

_____

_____

_____

_____

According to verses 7 through 9, whose positive example did Paul offer?

_____

_____

Now, read 3:10–15. What acts and attitudes did Paul condemn? What order did he give in verse 10?

_____

_____

_____

_____

What command did Paul give to those who were "leading an undisciplined life, doing no work at all, but acting like busybodies"?

_____

_____

_____

_____

What command did he give to those who observed other church members acting in a lazy or irresponsible manner? See verses 13–15.

_____

_____

_____

_____

Occupying our time wisely while we wait for Christ's return may take effort, but it's worth it! God rewards those who serve Him responsibly.

Purify

Second, _we must remember to purify ourselves as we prepare for the Lord's return._ Paul offers biblical support for this in Titus 2:11–14.

Read these verses. What has appeared? What does it bring to all mankind?

_____

_____

Why did Christ give Himself for us?

_____

_____

_____

_____

What is a telltale sign that a ministry has strayed from the truth? It emphasizes the Lord's return but fails to emphasize the importance of living a responsible, godly life in the meantime. We must demonstrate balanced thinking and behavior if we want to remain true to God's Word!

Now, read 1 John 3:1–3. What are we called? Why does the world not know us?

_____

_____

_____

_____

When Jesus appears, what will happen to us?

_____

_____

_____

_____

What should all people do who have their hope fixed on Jesus? Why?

_____

_____

_____

_____

Just as a bride purifies herself and prepares to walk down the aisle to meet her beloved groom, we as Christians are called to purify ourselves spiritually as the Bride of Christ to meet our Bridegroom when He returns for us. In light of what we *are* (3:1) and what we *will be* (3:2), John tells us what we *should do* (3:3): purify our lives by holy living.

Watch

In addition to the commands to occupy and purify, *we're exhorted to watch and prepare diligently for Christ's return.*

Read John 14:1–3. Who is speaking in this passage? What is promised here?

_____

_____

_____

_____

Now look at 15:16. What are we to do until He comes for us? Why do you think this is so significant?

_____

_____

_____

_____

The passion of Jesus's words is unmistakable, so isn't it remarkable that we often allow days, months, and even years to pass in which we barely give a moment's thought to the return of Christ? Yet, as spiritually sensitive people, we should be thinking about, praying about, and preparing for Christ's return. Jesus has called us to make disciples and to share the good news of salvation with people from every nation, tribe, and tongue. We must make sure that others are prepared to face the future with confidence that is based in an eternal relationship with Jesus Christ.

Think back to a time when you awaited the arrival of a date, a friend, a family member, or an honored guest at your home. As you waited for that person, how did your anticipation manifest itself? Maybe your heart started to beat faster or your stomach felt fluttery. Maybe you went to the door and peeked out over and over again, or you practically wore out the curtains from opening them to look outside so many times! You may have watched for headlights or waited anxiously to hear your guest's car turn into the drive. Maybe you even tried to pretend that you were reading a book or doing something else to pass the time, but in your heart, you knew that it was useless. All of your emotional and physical energy was focused on your guest's arrival.

Is that how you feel about Jesus's return?

Read 2 Timothy 4:7–8. According to verse 7, Paul wasn't sitting idle, wasting time as he waited for Jesus's return. What was he doing?

_____

_____

_____

_____

What has been laid up for Paul in the future? Who will award it to him?

_____

_____

_____

_____

According to verse 8, how did Paul feel about Jesus's appearing? How does this make you feel about your own anticipation and preparation for Christ's return?

_____

_____

_____

_____

Worship

Finally, *we're called to worship while we wait for Christ to return.* Sadly, we don't often hear much about the importance of worship as we await Christ's return, but Scripture places great emphasis on it. Worship is just as important to our spiritual preparation (if not more so) as occupying, purifying, and watching for the Lord's return.

We'll spend more time talking about the glorious privileges of worship in chapter 22, so we will focus on just a few aspects of worship in this chapter.

Read 1 Corinthians 11:23–26. How long are we, as Christians, supposed to participate in worship? How long are we to gather around the Lord's Table to take communion, solemnly considering the elements that symbolize our Savior's body and blood?

_____

_____

_____

_____

Every time we meet to share fellowship and worship with other believers, we're preparing for Christ's return. We're reminding ourselves and each other that Jesus will come again. Who knows? Maybe the worship experience you had last Sunday will be the last that you have on this earth. Maybe the communion that you took part in on Sunday will be your last. Every meal that we share at the Lord's Table reminds us that Christ's return is drawing near. We worship Him with great thankfulness for what He has done for us in the past, joy regarding what He's doing in the present, and anticipation for all He will do in the future.

In Case You Were Wondering

Q: How can I live daily with Christ's return in mind? How does this manifest itself practically in my life?

A: Paul gave us a hint in Philippians 1. Having expressed his thanks for the Philippians' financial support "from the first day until now" (1:5), Paul then expressed his conviction that they will continue to bear fruit until Christ's return: "For I am confident of this very thing, that He who began a good work in you will perfect it until the day of Christ Jesus" (1:6). Paul confirmed his confidence in God's continuance of the good work of spiritual growth in believers until the day of Christ.

We can maintain an awareness of our part in God's grand design by realizing that He has begun a good work in us and He will be faithful to complete it. We can either submit to or strive against the work that God wants to do in our lives. To the degree that we cooperate with Him, God will mold, shape, and sanctify us as believers until Christ returns. The same God who inspired the Philippian believers to give to Him will multiply the value of our fruit and our gifts until the day Christ returns! So let's be diligent in living godly lives, sharing the truth with others, and being unified in fellowship with one another until Christ returns to earth.

Digging Deeper

How to Stay Alert and Ready

Let's explore three simple ways we can stay alert and be ready for Christ's return:

1. *Remember* that Jesus promised He would return someday.

2. *Realize* that Jesus could return today.

3. *Apply* our marching orders: occupy, purify, watch, and worship.

Why do you think we often wait until a crisis point (an accident or injury, a divorce, the death of a friend, or another traumatic event) to soberly weigh our investments of time, money, energy, passion, and abilities?

_____

_____

_____

_____

If Jesus returned right now and asked you, His servant, to account for the "mina" He has given you, what would you say?

_____

_____

_____

_____

In what ways would you like to improve your stewardship? How could you better occupy, purify, watch, and worship?

_____

_____

_____

_____

Until Christ returns, focus your time and energy on living the full, godly, abundant life that God has promised you. Take your Bible or your journal and write down the four "watchwords" you've learned in this chapter. In addition, list one or two personal goals or ministry opportunities that you feel God is leading you toward. How can you make these goals a reality? Remember, time is short, and God has placed you on this earth for a reason! Make the most of the spiritual opportunities He's given you. Redeem your time!

SECTION NINE

RESURRECTION

17

VISITING THE <u>REAL</u> TWILIGHT ZONE

Selected Scriptures

"You are about to enter another dimension, a dimension not only of sight and sound but of mind. A journey into a wondrous land of imagination. Next stop, the Twilight Zone!" [1]

The late Rod Serling, who spoke these memorable words, had a creative way of helping his audience transition from the world of the seen to the unseen, out of the realm of the "now" into the frightening dimension called "The Twilight Zone." And that haunting music—only four notes in a minor key—certainly did evoke eerie emotions!

"The Twilight Zone" dealt specifically with death and the afterlife. One of the reasons for the show's success may be that people have always been strangely fascinated by thanatology—the study of death. Colleges everywhere offer courses, seminars, and dialogues on death and dying, grief, suicide, euthanasia, and "near-death" or "out-of-body" experiences. In addition, more recent TV shows such as "Six Feet Under," "Touched by an Angel," "Beyond," "The Medium," and "Revelations" demonstrate that modern viewers continue to have an interest in death, spirituality, the afterlife, and related phenomena.

DEATH: ITS INEVITABILITY AND EFFECT

We will all die. There's no escaping it. Sometimes, death occurs calmly and peacefully. At other times, it happens in a way that's heart-wrenching, violent, and ugly. Sometimes it seems to happen prematurely, tearing from our arms a tiny baby, a beloved spouse, or a young person in the prime of his or her life. On other occasions, death seems to hide its face even from those who long to be free from their physical pain or limitations. But, according to God's timing, physical death will occur for each of us. We can't avoid it.

Scripture speaks clearly and often about death. Here are just a few samples from God's Word.

> By the sweat of your face
> You will eat bread,
> Till you return to the ground,
> Because from it you were taken;
> For you are dust,
> And to dust you shall return. (Genesis 3:19)

> What man can live and not see death?
> Can he deliver his soul from the power of Sheol? (Psalm 89:48)

> Therefore, just as through one man sin entered into the world, and death through sin, . . . death spread to all men, because all sinned. (Romans 5:12)

> [I]t is appointed for men to die once and after this comes judgment. (Hebrews 9:27)

From Genesis to Revelation, the death knell sounds. Our appointment with death is the one appointment we have no choice but to keep.

Getting to the Root

Scripture uses several descriptive terms and euphemisms to refer to death. The primary Hebrew terms used for *death* are *muth* and *maveth*. David uses an unusual compound Hebrew term, *tsalmaveth*, in Psalm 23:4; 44:19; 107:10; and 107:14. This term, a combination of the Hebrew words *tsel* ("a shadow") and *maveth* ("death"), may be translated, "death-like shadow; deep shadow; black gloom; deep darkness; shadow of death." [2]

The Greek word *thanatos*, from which we derive the term *thanatology*, is translated, "death; danger of death; pestilence." [3] Paul uses this term liberally in his letters, especially in Romans, to compare sin under the Law (which leads to spiritual and physical death) with the Spirit of Christ, which brings us life and peace (see Romans 8:6).

The following legend illustrates the inevitability of death and man's inability to outsmart it:

> A merchant in Bagdad [*sic*] . . . one day sent his servant to the market. Before very long the servant came back, white and trembling, and in great agitation said to his master: "Down in the market place I was jostled by a woman in the crowd, and when I turned around I saw it was Death that jostled me. She looked at me and made a threatening gesture. Master, please lend me your horse, for I must hasten away to avoid her. I will ride to Samarra and there I will hide, and Death will not find me."
>
> The merchant lent him his horse and the servant galloped away in great haste. Later the merchant went down to the market place and saw Death standing in the crowd. He went over to her and asked, "Why did you frighten my servant this morning? Why did you make a threatening gesture?"
>
> "That was not a threatening gesture," Death said. "It was only a start of surprise. I was astonished to see him in Bagdad, for I have an appointment with him tonight in Samarra."[4]

Yes, we all have our own appointment in Samarra. Though we may try to avoid it, the appointment will not be canceled.

But what happens at death, when we have to keep that final appointment? What occurs exactly when life departs from the physical body? Let's turn to Scripture to find out.

RESURRECTION: PROMISES AND PROCEDURE

For Christians

First, let's address Christians—those who know they have eternal life with Jesus Christ. We exist in basically two parts: that which is seen (our body, our outer person) and that which is unseen (our inner person, our soul, our spirit). Let's think in these categories as we read 2 Corinthians 5:1–8.

What kind of a "house" do we currently inhabit? How is this house characterized?

_____

_____

_____

_____

What kind of "house" do we have from God? While we're at home in our physical bodies, whom are we absent from?

_____

_____

_____

_____

What are we called to walk by? What are we *not* called to walk by? What does this mean to you in light of your own spiritual walk and personal struggles?

_____

_____

_____

_____

What (and where) does Paul say he would prefer to be? What can we learn from his perspective?

_____

_____

_____

_____

We all know that while we're on this earth, our physical bodies "groan." Even when we're very young, we carry in our bodies the marks of sin, disease, and death. Our bodies were created to be eternal, and they long to be transformed into their glorified state. But as long as we're present in these fragile, aging bodies, we're absent from the physical presence of our Lord.

But what exactly *is* death? In one word, death means *separation*. When death occurs, the inner part of us is separated from the outer; the soul and spirit depart from the body. That is the simplest description of death—the moment when the soul and spirit, those elements that "animate" us as humans, leave the physical body. The physical part of us dies and immediately begins to decay. But, if we have trusted Christ for salvation, the inner part of us—the personality, the soul, the spirit—will be in the presence of the Lord.

Read 2 Corinthians 4:16–18. What is happening to the outer man? How does this contrast with what is happening to the inner man?

_____

_____

_____

_____

What is "momentary, light affliction" producing in us?

_____

_____

_____

_____

Compare 2 Corinthians 5:7 with 2 Corinthians 4:18. What similarities do you see? Why do you think Paul makes this repeated emphasis?

_____

_____

_____

_____

Keep in mind that death always means separation—an instant severance of the soul and spirit from the body. The physical body (whether cremated, buried, embalmed, or destroyed) remains on earth, while the soul and spirit depart to be with the Lord. Now, let's explore what happens to our physical bodies after we die.

Digging Deeper

The Glorification of the Body

The following two passages of Scripture deal with the glorification of our physical bodies. The first states the promise of the glorification of our bodies; the second explains the procedure involved in this glorification, which we examined in chapter 15 of this workbook.

> Knowing that He who raised the Lord Jesus will raise us also with Jesus and will present us with you.
> (2 Corinthians 4:14)

> For the Lord Himself will descend from heaven with a shout, with the voice of the archangel and with the trumpet of God, and the dead in Christ will rise first. Then we who are alive and remain will be caught up together with them in the clouds to meet the Lord in the air, and so we shall always be with the Lord.
> (1 Thessalonians 4:16–17)

When the death of the physical body takes place, the soul and spirit depart immediately into the presence of the Lord. There is no "soul sleep"; neither is there reincarnation or "reentry" into the physical body. Remember the example of the thief on the cross? Immediately after he pledged his faith in Christ, Jesus said to Him, "Truly I say to you, *today* you shall be with Me in Paradise" (Luke 23:43, emphasis added).

At the moment of physical death, our soul and spirit will enter instantly into the presence of the Lord to await the resurrection of the body. When the body is resurrected, the soul and spirit will be joined to that glorified body, which will no longer "groan," age, or suffer any of its former limitations. It will be fitted for eternity. And in this glorified state, we will spend forever with our God.

For Non-Christians

The New Testament has a lot to say about the future of the non-believer, as well. You may be surprised to find that the Bible discusses and describes hell more often (and in more detail) than it does heaven.

Read Matthew 23:25–33. To whom is Jesus speaking? How would you describe His tone? What strong warning does He offer in verse 33?

_____

_____

_____

_____

Now, turn to Matthew 25:31–33. According to verse 32, who will be gathered before the Son of Man? How will He separate them?

_____

_____

_____

_____

Now, read 25:34–40. What did the King say to those on his right? What questions did the righteous ask the Lord in verses 37 through 39?

_____

_____

_____

_____

According to verse 40, what response did the King give? Though your salvation is secure if you have trusted Christ, consider the current level of love, mercy, hospitality, and help you are offering to others. In which of these areas do you need to grow?

_____

_____

_____

_____

Now, read verses 32–33 and 41–46. What will Christ say to those on His left? What has been prepared for the "goats" as well as for the devil and his angels?

_____

_____

_____

_____

To whom should you be providing food, fellowship, clothing, financial help, or assistance as a reflection of your commitment to Christ? List at least one specific person who could use your help, and consider a particular way that you could minister to him or her *this week*. Then, do it! Also, think about how you can make this type of ministry a regular part of your life rather than just a one-time project.

_____

_____

_____

_____

If you feel apprehensive after reading these passages, or if you fear that you may hear Christ say the words, "Depart from Me," perhaps you've never established a true, saving relationship with God by placing your faith in Jesus Christ. If you'd like to find out more about developing a relationship with the Lord, please turn to the section titled "How to Begin a Relationship with God" in the back of this workbook.

In Case You Were Wondering

Q: I don't have a clear picture of what heaven will be like. What descriptions of heaven does Scripture provide?

A: As children, we tend to fear that heaven will be just like an endless church service. But our childhood conception of eternity with God falls far short of the Bible's glorious description of heaven.

The concept of some kind of eternal bliss is universal, but the heaven described in the Bible is not simply a culmination of our *human* hopes and desires. It won't be "whatever you love the most" or "whatever you want it to be." It's not a place in which all of your earthly, physical wants, desires, and pleasures will be fulfilled.

The biblical term *heaven* refers to the state of being in the presence of the Lord and experiencing His everlasting blessing. After our physical death, we who know Christ will live forever in His presence and in the company of the elect angels and the believers who have died before us.

Interestingly, many of the biblical attributes and descriptions of heaven are also attributes of God Himself. For example, heaven is characterized by the following:

- *Glory* (see Isaiah 6:3; John 17:24; Revelation 21:23; Romans 8:18; Colossians 3:4; 1 Peter 1:7)

- *Holiness* (see Isaiah 57:15; 6:3; Revelation 21:27)

- *Beauty* (see Psalm 50:2; 8:1; Isaiah 33:17; Revelation 21:10–11)

- *Immortality* (see 1 Timothy 1:17; Isaiah 9:6–7; Micah 5:2; John 8:58; 1 Corinthians 15:53–54; Revelation 21:4)

- *Light* (see Isaiah 60:1, 19; John 8:12; Revelation 21:23)

- *Perfection* (see Psalm 18:30; Deuteronomy 32:4; 2 Samuel 22:31; Matthew 5:48; 1 Corinthians 13:9–10, 12; 1 John 3:2)

- *Love* (see 1 John 4:8; 1 Corinthians 13:8, 13)

- *Joy* (see Zephaniah 3:17; Isaiah 62:4–5; 65:17–19; Revelation 19:6–7) [5]

From Scripture, we can also determine what heaven is *not*. In our new dwelling place, there will be no time and no sin (Revelation 21:27), no sun, moon, or sea (21:1, 23), no curse (22:3), and, best of all, no suffering or sorrow (21:4).

In heaven, we will recognize our friends and loved ones, as well as the saints of Scripture—men and women like Abraham, Sarah, Moses, Esther, David, Mary, Peter, Ruth, and Paul. We will be joyfully occupied in worship and service. We have only a short time left in this life; let's redeem that time in the best possible way by engaging in worship, instruction, fellowship, evangelism, and service.

PREPARATION: RESPONSE AND RESULT

In our study of this chapter, we have come to two important conclusions about death. First, *the only time that we can prepare for death is now, before it happens.* God created us as eternal creatures, so we all will have eternal life. We just have to choose where we're going to spend it! An eternity with God will mean unmatched bliss, the disappearance of all pain and sadness, and perfect, unmarred fellowship with the Father, Son, and Holy Spirit. An eternity in hell, on the other hand, means separation from God and the unimaginable horrors of spiritual and physical agony that will never cease. It doesn't seem like a difficult choice, does it?

The second fact we must remember is that *we'll have no chance to change our spiritual status after death.* Scripture contains no references to a place called "purgatory"—a sort of "spiritual waiting room" where the souls of the dead wait to be "prayed into heaven" by friends and family members. There's no such place! Establishing a relationship with God through Jesus Christ is *your* responsibility; no one can do it for you. When you appear before God, He'll ask you to account for your own spiritual state and the activities that you engaged in on earth. Your parents, spouse, children, mentor, or pastor will not be asked to account for your choices; *you will.* And for those without Christ, the judgment will be condemnation. Wouldn't you rather establish a true, saving relationship with Jesus Christ, who died and rose from the dead in order to redeem you from your sins and grant you eternal life with God?

The distinctive voice of Rod Serling fell silent when he, too, passed away and entered "The Twilight Zone" of the afterlife. We don't know whether he chose to spend eternity with God or not, but he did have that choice, and you do too. Take a good, hard look at your life right now. Will you hear Jesus welcome you home when you leave this life and enter the next?

18

An Interview with One from Beyond
Luke 16

In the 2005 Terri Schiavo case, a fierce "right-to-live" court battle raged between the parents of a brain-damaged woman, who wanted to keep her alive, and her husband, who wanted to have her feeding tube removed. Eventually, the Supreme Court ordered that Schiavo's feeding tube be removed at her husband's request—against her parents' wishes and to the chagrin of Schiavo's staunch supporters. Schiavo died a week or so later. This woman's heartbreaking case paved the way for people all over the world to ask difficult questions about life and death and to try to come to terms with their own mortality.

Ultimate Realities for Non-Christians to Face

In the book of Luke, we find an extremely vivid and rare account in which a *non-Christian* is interviewed after death. This startling afterlife narrative is related by the ultimate authority on the subject—Jesus, the Son of God Himself.

Some commentators refer to Luke 16:19–31 as a parable, but, by naming two of the key characters in the account, Jesus could be relating these verses as an actual historical event. Regardless, Jesus assumes the *setting* of the story as true.

Luke sets the stage in 16:19–22. Read these verses. How is the rich man characterized in life? What material blessings did he have?

_____

_____

_____

_____

How is the poor man, Lazarus, characterized in life?

_____

_____

_____

_____

According to verse 22, what happened to the poor man immediately after his death?

_____

_____

_____

_____

What happened to the rich man after his death?

_____

_____

_____

_____

When Lazarus died, his body was probably tossed in the local dump, but his spirit immediately entered what's called "Abraham's bosom"—a reference to the Old Testament saints' paradise prior the ascension of Christ to heaven. The rich man also died, and we can be sure that his burial ceremony was elaborate as his body was embalmed with spices and laid in an expensive tomb. But what happened to his *spirit*?

Read 16:23–24. How is Hades described? What did the rich man ask Abraham for?

_____

_____

_____

_____

According to verses 25 and 26, Abraham gave two reasons why Lazarus could not fulfill the rich man's wishes. What were they?

_____

_____

_____

_____

Getting to the Root

The word translated "chasm" in Luke 16:26 appears only twice in Scripture. It first appears in Jeremiah 48:28 as the translation of the Hebrew word *pachath*, meaning "a pit, cave, or chasm." The Greek word *chasma* comes from the word *chaskō*, which literally means "to yawn." This word is translated as "a chasm or wide space."[1] The chasm that divided the rich man from the poor man represented both a literal (physical) and figurative (spiritual) distance that could never be crossed.

The "fixed chasm" referred to in 16:26 suggests an unchangeable situation. In other words, we can't change our eternal destiny (or our destination) after death. Realizing this, the rich man began to try to bargain with Abraham.

According to 16:27–28, what did the rich man want Lazarus to do?

_____

_____

_____

_____

What response did Abraham give?

_____

_____

_____

_____

How does the rich man's experience make you feel about those people you know who do not have a relationship with Jesus Christ?

_____

_____

_____

_____

Have you ever thought about the idea that the lost who are dead agonize over the lost who are alive? Because the rich man was unable to escape, his number-one concern was that someone might go to his brothers and communicate the truth about his torment to those who were living. Don't miss the urgency—"that he may warn them." Talk about a missionary message! Talk about zeal for sharing the truth that Christ has a much better offer for us! If it exists nowhere else, an evangelistic passion exists in Hades. "Oh, I wish that someone could go to my parents, my brothers and sisters, and my children! If only someone could share the truth with my loved ones who are living just like I lived, denying what I denied."

Jesus's teaching on hell certainly silences those who joke, "Oh, I'll just be in hell with all my buddies." The Bible never describes hell as a place of fellowship. On the contrary, those in hell will experience utter loneliness, agony, torture, thirst, pain, and an eternal, horrific knowledge that they denied Christ and failed to believe the truth set forth in God's Word.

Now, let's get back to our story. In response to the rich man's request, Abraham said to him, "They have Moses and the prophets." Meaning what? They have the Scripture, the very Word of God. In other words, "Let those who are alive hear the truth of the Scripture. They have ample opportunity to hear the truth." In our day, people can pick up the Bible and read it for themselves. They can listen to preachers. They can hear Christian radio broadcasts. They can understand the gospel as it is contained in God's Word.

Scripture has so much power. If you could bring someone back from beyond—someone destined for hell—to tell people what the future holds, even that would not be as effective as Holy Scripture! The soul-piercing, convicting power of the Word of God through the Holy Spirit changes lives.

FIVE MAJOR QUESTIONS WORTH ANSWERING

Before we leave this section on resurrection, let's consider several significant concerns.

How can a loving God send people to hell?

This question seems to imply that by sending sinners to hell, God is treating mankind unfairly. Some seem to believe that God takes delight in saying, "Get out of my sight," as He pushes people into hell against their will. Suffice it to say, that is *not* what Scripture teaches about our merciful God.

God is loving, without a doubt. But that's not all! He's also holy and just, and He cannot allow sin to remain unpunished. On the cross of Christ, the love of God and the justice of God met—and both were satisfied. God demonstrated His love by providing a way for our sins to be forgiven. God also satisfied His justice in punishing all sin through Christ's sacrifice.

God's divine rule states that those who believe in His Son will have eternal life with Him, and those who do not believe in His Son will not have eternal life with Him. The same God who will send people to hell sent His own Son to the cross so that no one *has* to go to hell, if they will only choose to believe in Christ. Those who reject the message of salvation through Jesus Christ's sacrifice, on the other hand, must face the dire consequences of that rejection.

 God is far from being callous and unconcerned about the future of the lost. Return to 2 Peter 3:9. How is God described in this passage? What is His desire?

_____

_____

_____

_____

Never forget that verse! When someone presents to you the idea that God cruelly and gleefully dances around heaven as the last people are dumped into hell against their will, remind that person of Peter's words. With patience and grace, our Father offers the gift of eternal life to all who will accept it. Those who refuse the gift He offers must suffer the consequences, having made their own decision about eternity.

What about those who have never heard? And what about those people who sincerely follow their own beliefs and their own religion, which they believe to be true?

If God would not condemn those who have never heard, then we would have no need for missionary programs. But, in the Great Commission, Jesus clearly commanded believers to "Go and make disciples of all nations." In Romans 1:18–22, we find God's wrath revealed not against "those who haven't heard," but against all sinners. Rather than asking, *Why aren't they saved?* the Bible asks, *Why are they lost?* People don't die for lack of a doctor; they die because they're sick. Also, Romans 1:19–22 says that mankind has suppressed the truth it *does* have. People are "without excuse" when they see God's love and divine plan revealed in creation and refuse to respond to Him. If someone does respond, God will give him or her further revelation—namely, the gospel (see Acts 8 and 10). People will not be condemned for not hearing the truth; instead, they will be condemned for ignoring the God that creation affirms and for violating their own moral standards—their own consciences (see Romans 2:14–15).

As far as other religions are concerned, the real issue is: "Is God holy?" Because if God is holy and if the principles in His Word are true, then a person can have salvation only through faith in Christ. If God is holy, then anyone who seeks to "bribe" Him by moral payment or any other means appalls Him.

All other religions seek to receive God's favor through good works.

Sinners don't need long lists of made-up rules to follow; they need a Savior. Outside Christianity, no faith addresses the problem of how to deal with sin in the face of a holy God. If Christianity says we're saved not by works but by grace—and all other religions say we're saved by works—either one religious group is wrong, all of them are wrong, or all of them are wrong *but one.* Jesus said, "No one comes to the Father but through Me" (John 14:6).

What about deathbed repentance?

We've all heard about people who profess faith in Christ during their last hours or even their final minutes on earth. They've spent their entire life apart from faith in the Lord Jesus and now, as they are dying, they express strong and confident faith in the Lord. Is this faith valid?

We must remember that no one on earth can determine with absolute certainty the eternal destiny of another individual, since God alone knows the heart. But who is to say that no one can become a Christian at the end of his or her life? Remember the penitent thief on the cross? He had lived the life of a criminal. He had lived his entire life without trusting in Christ. But in his final breath, he demonstrated faith in Jesus and made a strong statement regarding eternity, and Christ acknowledged it.

We must be careful about expecting people to say the exact words we want to hear so we can say to them in return, "Now you're a Christian." Be careful about giving them the prayer that they must recite or the exact words that they must repeat. Who can say for sure what language the heart speaks when one "believes in his heart that Jesus is Lord"? The thief on the cross said, "Jesus, remember me when You come into Your kingdom," and in his case, those words were sufficient. The Lord read the language of the thief's heart. After all, it's faith that saves — not prayer.

What about the death of babies?

This question is extremely important to those who have lost a young child who never reached an age of spiritual comprehension. Scripture seems to indicate that small children who die before reaching a certain level of maturity (when they are able to understand the basic issues of salvation and faith in Christ) go immediately into the presence of the Lord.

No passage of Scripture is more clear on this subject than 2 Samuel 12:23 RSV, where David says of his infant who has just died, "I shall go to him, but he will not return to me." In addition to affirming the permanence of death, David affirmed his expectation of fellowship with his son. God has reserved a place in heaven for the precious infants and children whose lives ended prematurely on this earth. David stated the truth as he testified to the inability of his baby to return to earth. But David knew that when he himself died, he would see his child again once he entered the presence of the Lord.

In St. Andrew's churchyard in Scotland, an epitaph engraved on a tombstone echoes the profound theology of Romans 5:12–21 in simple terms:

> Bold infidelity, turn pale and die.
> Beneath this stone four sleeping infants lie:
> Say, are they lost or saved?
> If death's by sin, they sinned, for they are here.
> If heaven's by works, in heaven they can't appear,
> Reason, ah, how depraved!
> Turn to the Bible's sacred page, the knot's untied:
> They died, for Adam sinned; they live, for Jesus died.[2]

Is reincarnation valid?

Reincarnation is not valid according to Scripture. The Bible consistently refers to the death of an individual as a singular event. Hebrews 9:27 says, "It is appointed for men to die *once* and after this comes judgment" (emphasis added). And don't forget the "great chasm fixed" that we read earlier in Luke 16:26. Once death occurs, a fixed destiny has been determined and cannot be changed.

The concept of reincarnation is based on *karma*, the belief that through a series of lives one becomes a better and better person until he or she reaches a state of spiritual perfection called *nirvana*. However, if you and I could attain perfection on our own, we wouldn't need Christ! Scripture says that all of us *do* need Christ. We cannot save ourselves. We've been given only one life to live on this earth, and our salvation depends on us choosing to follow Christ during that lifetime. There's no possibility of reincarnation.

In Case You Were Wondering

Q: If a Christian commits suicide, will he or she go to heaven? How does this relate to the passage in Matthew 12 in which Jesus says that "blaspheming the Holy Spirit" is the only unforgivable sin?

A: Many ideas have been suggested as to what Jesus meant by "blaspheming the Holy Spirit." Perhaps the most common theory is that God will not forgive one who refuses to believe in Jesus Christ for salvation. But Jesus seemed to mean something more specific than a broad general reference because, without salvation through faith alone in Jesus Christ, *all* sins remain unpardonable.

Jesus made the well-known statement about "blaspheming the Holy Spirit" in Matthew 12:31–32 in response to the Pharisees' accusation that He cast out demons by the power of the devil rather than by the power of the Holy Spirit. The unpardonable sin Jesus spoke of appears in a context of Him offering the long-awaited kingdom of God to Israel, while validating His offer through miracles done by the power of the Holy Spirit. Notice His words, "But if I cast out demons by the Spirit of God, *then the kingdom of God has come upon you*" (12:28, emphasis added). The religious leaders committed blasphemy of the Spirit by attributing Jesus's incredible messianic miracles to the devil. And if they persisted in this view, the sin would be unforgivable in that the promised kingdom would not appear in that generation—and it didn't.

According to this interpretation, no one in the present can commit the "unforgivable sin" (blasphemy of the Spirit), for Jesus is not physically here on earth today doing miracles by the Holy Spirit. The sin was restricted to Jesus's offer of the kingdom to first-century Israel.

Many erroneously associate suicide with the unpardonable sin. An often-misunderstood verse comes from 1 Corinthians 3:17: "If any man destroys the temple of God, God will destroy him, . . ." But the rest of the verse explains, "for the temple of God is holy, and that is what you are." The "you" in the original Greek is plural, referring to the church as a body, and the context also indicates that the "temple" spoken of here is the church, not an individual's life or body.

Suicide is a sin, true, but so are homicide, infanticide, and genocide—all tragic and terrible (and sometimes premeditated) deaths. But consider this question: is there any sin that Christ's death on the cross can't cover? Isn't He able to forgive murderers? Just look at the examples of David and Paul. Both of these men participated in the sinful murders of individuals during their lifetimes, yet God forgave them. Did Jesus die for all sins except suicide? According to the Bible, faith in Jesus Christ is *the only qualification for heaven*. Therefore, suicide in itself does not disqualify a person from heaven if, at a previous point in time, that person truly placed his or her faith in Christ for salvation.

Where Will You Spend Eternity?

Sadly, America is still largely a culture that has rejected Christ, especially in the postmodern, politically correct twenty-first century. How tragic! When we refuse to believe that death will happen or that we will be called to account for our actions, we're in trouble. Whenever we're tempted to focus on the things of this life and put off eternal issues, we can remember the life of the rich man that Jesus described.

What is your spiritual status? If you've already accepted Christ, think about your family and friends. Do you have loved ones who need to hear the life-transforming message of salvation through Christ *now*, before it's too late? If so, don't wait. Be the first to demonstrate God's love to those people by sharing with them how they, too, can have eternal life by placing their faith in Jesus Christ.

SECTION TEN

The Body of Christ

19

GOD'S BODY-BUILDING PROGRAM
Selected Scriptures

To many people, attending church is like watching a show. The better the entertainment, the more they enjoy attending. But if the worship service starts to get less entertaining, many people will stop showing up! They expect good, solid entertainment in exchange for the dollar that they drop into the offering plate each week.

All of this is true, of course, until we start to get serious about the church. When we grow to *love* the church as we should, we will want to invest our time and our treasure into doing God's work. We'll concentrate more on what we have to give than on what the church has to give us. And it's not long before we realize that the church is one of the few entities that offers us a multitude of earthly blessings as well as eternal rewards.

A DEFINITION OF THE CHURCH

We could define the church as "the ever-enlarging body of born-again believers who comprise the universal body of Christ over whom He reigns as Lord." Can you think of anything more worthy of your time and treasure? When you catch a vision for the church and develop a passion for living with an eternal perspective rather than just expecting a "pretty good show for a dollar," your entire frame of reference will shift. You'll see the church as a worldwide, invincible movement over which Christ serves as Lord. And you'll realize that your part in it is vital!

Prediction of the Church

The term "church" appears late in Scripture. It doesn't show up at all in the Old Testament, and it's not mentioned in the New Testament until Christ's ministry is well underway. Jesus mentioned the church toward the end of a dialogue between Himself and His disciples in Matthew 16:13–18. Take a moment to read this passage.

Jesus directed His question toward the group — the "you" in verse 15 is plural. But Peter alone answered the question, and his answer was right on target! According to verse 16, whom did Peter say Jesus was?

_____

_____

_____

_____

According to verse 17, who revealed this answer to Peter?

_____

_____

_____

_____

In Matthew 16:17–18, Jesus offers a threefold response to Peter's answer: first a blessing, then a promise, and finally a prediction. Look carefully at Jesus's blessing: "Blessed are you, Simon Barjona, because flesh and blood did not reveal this to you, but My Father who is in heaven." Next came the giving of a new name: "I also say to you that you are Peter [*Petros*], . . ." That must have been wonderful for Peter to hear! Jesus gave him a personal, meaningful nickname. All of his life, Peter had been known as *Simon*, which means "vacillating one, shifting, moody, changing." But *Petros* meant "Rock." In effect, Christ says, "Good job, Rock. Way to go!"

Then, drawing on that nickname, Jesus makes a promise: "And upon this *Petra* I will build My church; . . ." *Petra* is not quite the same word as *Petros*. Some have taught that this passage means Jesus built His church on Peter, but it doesn't. Jesus built His church on the *Petra*—the rock-like truth Peter had just uttered. And what is this truth? Peter's proclamation that "You are the Messiah, the Anointed One, the Son of the Living God."

Now, read verse 18 for the prediction. Jesus said, ". . . and the gates of Hades will not overpower [My church]." The church is not built by some pastor or priest or body of elders or some other governing hierarchy. It is Jesus who builds it. The church is solely His. He doesn't have to clear His decisions with the Vatican or any other entity. As the Savior and the Bridegroom, He has the authority over His Bride, the church (Ephesians 5:22–32).

Getting to the Root

The word *church* comes from the Greek term *ekklesia*, which is a combination of the words *ek*, a prefix particle meaning "out from among," and *klesia*, from the verb *kaleo*, meaning "to call." Combining the two terms, *ekklesia* means "to call out from among." To render Jesus's prediction literally, we would say, "I will build My called-out ones."[1]

Since the beginning of the church, our Lord has been reaching down into the ranks of humanity, calling people to Himself: men, women, boys, girls—people with all different personalities from every nation, tongue, and tribe. He continues to "call them out," and He places each one of them in His body—the church.

The body is exclusive, in the right sense. The only way you can become a member of this body is to place your complete trust in Jesus Christ. If you're a believer, you're in! And even if all the forces of evil were unleashed from the open gates of Hades itself, the growth of the church would not be stopped. Satan may attempt to limit the effectiveness of the church by deceiving and misleading believers, but he will never be able to tear down what Christ has built. The church is a permanent entity, and it will never be destroyed.

In Case You Were Wondering

Q: Is it really necessary for me to attend church?

A: In a word, yes! One story tells of a pastor who went to visit a member of his congregation who had withdrawn from the church for no apparent reason. The pastor entered the man's house and sat with him by the fireplace, not saying a word. After a few minutes of silence, the pastor walked over to the fire, picked up the poker, and drew one of the burning logs out of the flames and set it down on the floor by itself. Then he sat down and waited. That log, burning brightly only moments before, began to cool. Soon it sat cold on the tile, with only a blackened crust to give any evidence it had ever been on fire at all. Without uttering a sound, the pastor rose from his seat and left the man's home.

The former church member got the message loud and clear: when a person is isolated from the body of Christ, his or her spiritual flame quickly dies out.

Too often, we view church attendance as identical to school or work attendance: we go because we have to, or because we think we will "get in trouble" if we don't. The truth is, the Bible doesn't say anything at all about dressing up and driving to a particular building one morning out of the week or about having perfect Sunday-school attendance. What it *does* say, however, is that when we join the family of God, new life awaits us. But that new life in all its abundance requires mutual encouragement, teaching, support, prayer, accountability, and fellowship with the rest of the church family.

Like a burning log removed from the fire, we'll lose the life and energy of our relationship with God if we remove ourselves from fellowship with other Christians. The author of Hebrews wrote,

"Let us consider how to stimulate one another to love and good deeds, not forsaking our own assembling together, as is the habit of some, but encouraging one another; and all the more as you see the day drawing near" (10:24–25). Don't give up on meeting with other Christians! If you do, you'll miss out on the vital blessings of teaching, worship, and fellowship that will help lead you into greater spiritual maturity.

THE RAPID GROWTH OF THE EARLY CHURCH

Let's observe how rapidly the body expanded in its earliest years of existence. When the Holy Spirit descended on the day of Pentecost, He ignited a small body of believers with enthusiasm and holy zeal. They poured out into the streets of Jerusalem and fearlessly declared their faith. "Petros" became their spokesman, and the immediate results were nothing short of phenomenal!

Read Acts 2:41–42. How many new believers were added that day? What did they continually devote themselves to?

_____

_____

_____

_____

These people stood there in the streets of Jerusalem with no church building, no pastor, no board of elders, and no "church constitution" (which is probably the reason why they got along so well!). But they did have Christ, and they also had each other. The ties of love held them closely together. As these new believers devoted themselves to carrying out the mission and the ordinances of the church, the body began to grow both in maturity and in numbers.

Read Acts 5:12–14. What contradictory responses did people have to the apostles' actions?

_____
_____
_____
_____

According to Acts 6:7, who was becoming obedient to the faith? What was significant about this fact?

_____
_____
_____
_____

Finally, because of persecution, the growth of the body extended beyond Jerusalem. Read Acts 11:19–24. Who received the Word at first? Who later received it?

_____
_____
_____
_____

How is Barnabas described? How can you follow his example in your own small group or church?

_____
_____
_____
_____

We've seen televised pictures of volcanoes that have erupted with enormous force, causing molten lava to pour over the lip of the crater and run down the crevices and into the valley and villages below. Wherever the lava flows, it leaves its mark. In the early church, the heat of persecution drove Christians into new regions, leading to further growth.

Just as Christ had predicted, the "gates of Hades" did not overpower the church. On the contrary, considerable numbers of people were brought to the Lord. But the growth didn't stop there. It continued into Greece and then throughout Europe. Lives were changed drastically as Christ's message penetrated and permeated the area. We see this clearly when we read the events that transpired in Ephesus, a metropolitan center in western Turkey.

Read Acts 19:17–20. What was happening to the name of the Lord? What do you think it would mean for us to do the same thing today?

_____

_____

_____

_____

How did these new believers demonstrate their commitment to life change?

_____

_____

_____

_____

What a remarkable account! How could pagan people have been changed so completely? Their radical transformation involved so much more than simply "joining a church." These changes occurred because Christ had invaded their hearts and completely changed their lives.

Digging Deeper

Two Changes That Occur When We Believe

When we make that crucial decision to trust Jesus Christ as our Savior, two vital things happen:

1. Something happens *within* us. According to 2 Corinthians 5:17, we become an entirely new creation. We gain new motivations and new interests. Our interests begin to shift from ourselves to others—from the things of the flesh to the things of God. And a new group of people appears on the horizon of our lives—other Christians. We begin to be more vulnerable, more open, and more willing to confess our sin. Our desire to hide from God changes to a desire to spend more time with Him. Why? We become new creatures within.

2. Something happens *to* us. When we express our faith in Christ, we instantaneously enter the family of God. We may not feel any different at that exact moment, but something vital happens the moment we believe. We become a part of God's forever family.

When we choose to trust God, we become new creatures, and we join God's family. And those two factors never change!

VITAL SIGNS OF A HEALTHY CHURCH

Sometimes people ask, "Do I have to join a church to become a Christian?" No, but once you become a Christian, God *wants* you to join a local church for teaching and fellowship. You automatically become a member of the universal body, His church, when you believe. No problem there. Usually, the problems begin to occur when we join a local church made up of fallible people just like us. Attending church should be a joyful and uplifting experience, but it may not be if that church's vital signs of health and wholeness are missing.

Let's explore the six signs of a healthy church that are mentioned or implied in 1 Corinthians 12.

First, *the presence of unity and harmony.* Read 1 Corinthians 12:12. See the unity and harmony of the body? Though the church is comprised of many members, it still consists of only one body.

Another sign of good church health is *the absence of favoritism, status, and prejudice.* Read 1 Corinthians 12:13. What are we all baptized into?

_____

_____

In the first-century Roman world, showing favoritism within the church was extremely common. At that time, a definite caste system existed. Some people were nobles, many of whom were slave owners. Other people were poverty-stricken, and many of them were slaves. A slave was treated as nothing more than a possession or a human "tool" in the hands of his or her master.

A healthy church, however, will treat people differently—it will not show favoritism among its members. God loves each of us equally. We have no basis for treating some people like "preferred customers" and others as "second-class citizens."

A third vital sign is *an emphasis on individual dignity and mutual variety.* We find this vital sign in verses 14–20. As you read this passage, don't miss Paul's tongue-in-cheek humor!

What part of the body would you say you are? How is your role vital to the functioning and health of the body?

_____

_____

_____

Can you picture an "eye-body"—one massive, six-foot eye? How useless and unattractive! The same could be said for an "ear-body." The point is so ridiculous that it's humorous. Unfortunately, our culture tends to exalt certain people who possess more visible gifts, making them stars and celebrities and putting them up on pedestals. But they're just eyes and ears! No one person in the body is the whole body. Let's stop making people our idols and worship only God instead. Sure, we need heroes, people we admire and love and respect. But we don't need six-foot eyeballs!

Sometimes, you may feel that your part of the body isn't as important as other parts. You may be the foot. Is the foot important? You bet! If you've ever had a rock in your shoe, you know how important the foot is. And women who wear high heels know that when their feet hurt, they can barely concentrate on anything else! Feet are vitally important to the body, and so is every other part.

Now we're ready for the fourth vital sign: *a de-emphasis on independence and self-sufficiency.* Listen to this, you self-sufficient, strong, and natural leaders! Pay attention, all of you entrepreneurs! Hear ye, hear ye, all of you independent-minded Lone Rangers! Read 1 Corinthians 12:21–23.

In your church, which roles would you say are considered "more honorable" and which are considered "less honorable"?

How does Paul emphasize the vital importance of every part of the body? How does this change your attitude and behavior toward those members whose gifts are often deemed "less honorable"?

The health of the whole body rests on the functioning of each small part. We're interdependent; we depend on each other for our very life.

This brings us to the fifth vital sign: *the support of others, whether they are hurting or being honored.*

Read 12:25–26. According to this passage, what attributes characterize a healthy church body?

_____

_____

_____

In a healthy church, if someone is hurting, you feel the sting of his or her pain. If someone can't keep up, you slow down and encourage him or her. If someone else is honored, you applaud and cheer with genuine joy. You rejoice when others rejoice and weep when they weep. That's what it means to be in a healthy church body.

Take a few moments to think about your own church body. In which areas is your church operating well as a body? In which areas does it need improvement?

_____

_____

_____

Sixth and last: *exaltation of Christ as Head and supreme authority.* Read verse 27.

Think about the significance of Christ's physical body through-out His birth, ministry, death, and resurrection. What does it mean for us (the church) to be Christ's "body"?

_____

_____

_____

Because we are fellow members of the body, we must apply ourselves to achieving mutual harmony. Spiritual disease can diminish the effectiveness of the body, so we must maintain habits of health and a consistent program of exercise in harmony with God's plan. How can you be a more vital, integral part of God's body-building program?

20

THREE CHEERS FOR THE CHURCH

Selected Scriptures

A young boy once asked his mother, "Mom, what's the highest number you've ever counted to?"

"I don't know. How about you?"

"I've counted all the way up to 5,372."

"Oh," said his mother. "Why did you stop there?"

"Church was over." [1]

Many people remember the churches of their childhood as places with stained glass and worn carpet — a building where kids had to be quiet, and where everything smelled old. For some, the word "church" evokes precious memories; for others, like the young boy above, the place seems less than exciting.

Do you remember the churches you attended or visited during *your* childhood? Picture yourself sitting there in the sanctuary, dwarfed by adults, outfitted with a suit and clip-on tie or a pink dress and patent-leather shoes. What memories or emotions come to mind when you think about your early church experiences? Jot down three one-or-two-word answers.

_____

_____

_____

The Best of Times

Whether you have positive or negative early memories of church, you'll probably never forget one vital aspect of your church experience — the people. A recent Gallup survey revealed that fellowship and community play a vital role in helping church-goers grow spiritually and be involved in their local churches. For example:

- Those with a best friend in their church are 21 percent more likely to be regular weekly attendees.

- Outwardly observed spiritual commitment is 15 percent greater among those who have a best friend in their church.

- 20 percent of those with a best friend in their church are more likely to say that faith is involved in every aspect of their lives.

George Gallup, Jr., said, "The connections we've discovered between human friendships, spiritual maturity, church satisfaction, and even feelings of intimacy with God are absolutely remarkable. Belonging comes before believing."[2]

Read Philippians 1:3–6, and consider Paul's words to his friends at Philippi. In what ways did Paul's friendship and love for these dear friends flow from the apostle's pen?

_____

_____

_____

_____

As we think about the churches of our childhoods, most of us can easily recall the bad parts: listening to long, dreary sermons; wearing uncomfortable clothes; and spending what seemed like an entire day at church every week. But what about the treasured memories? What about the times of joy? Paul *thanked God* when he remembered the Philippians (see 1:3).

Think about your early church experiences. Who had a positive spiritual influence on you? Write at least two names below.

_____

_____

_____

_____

Why did these people have such an influence on you? What did they say or do that impressed or encouraged you?

_____

_____

_____

_____

More than likely, these individuals influenced your life because God used them either to begin "a good work in you" or to "perfect it until the day of Christ Jesus" (1:6). Make no mistake, *God* began the work and *God* will complete it. But God uses significant people to accomplish His desires and to do His good work in our lives.

The Worst of Times

It may seem strange, but even on our most difficult days, we remember the people God has placed in our lives, and that helps lighten our load. And, surprisingly, we can give thanks even for the painful trials that come our way.

Now, read Philippians 1:7–8. Paul wrote these words from a Roman prison cell, yet he remembered the Philippians with joy and affection! Why? Because their love and encouragement greatly contributed to Paul's life and ministry.

We give thanks for the hard times not because we desire pain, but because pain and affliction bring people into our lives who are willing to love and comfort us. Many times, these are people whom we never would have known apart from our struggle. Perhaps you are single again after many years of marriage, or maybe you've lost a job, or experienced the death of a spouse or family member. Can you imagine facing such sorrows and disappointments without the fellowship of Christian friends?

When the church is operating as it should, your Christian brothers and sisters should love you free of charge—from the heart. Nobody should have to make them bring you meals, comfort you with a kind word, hold your hand in prayer, and listen to your troubles with compassion. They should want to! God wants to use the church to carry you through all your seasons of life—and to make you more like Christ.

Name at least one person in your life who has stood by you in difficult times.

_____

_____

_____

_____

In what situations did this person (or these people) help or comfort you? How did their fellowship help you during these times?

_____

_____

_____

_____

Charles Spurgeon said:

> Communion is strength; solitude is weakness. Alone, the fine old beech [tree] yields to the blast and lies prone on the meadow. In the forest, supporting each other, the trees laugh at the hurricane. The sheep of Jesus flock together. The social element is the genius of Christianity.[3]

God uses the love of simple, faithful Christian people to pour into our lives what we would never receive otherwise.

Read Philippians 1:9–11. Paul lists several benefits of Christians living out their love for each other. What are they?

_____

_____

_____

_____

As we've seen, our early impressions often set the mold for how our thoughts develop in the future. And while our impressions of church come from years of attending, we must also look to the Word of God—not simply our own experience—to fully understand God's intentions for the role of the church.

THE CHURCH'S SIGNIFICANCE—*SO WHAT?*

In spite of the imperfections of its people and programs, we should all stand and give three cheers for the church! The church does more than make memories. It offers us more than just a place to get married and buried. And it ministers to many more people than just those who meet regularly within the walls of the church building. Through the best and worst of times, God uses the church to minister to people on three levels, and each level gets a well-deserved cheer.

Cheer Number One: The Church's Significance in the World

On Sunday, September 9, 2001, churches across America recorded average attendance. But one week later, 25% more people flocked to churches throughout the country.[4] The national and international state of affairs following the September 11th attacks on the United States sparked questions regarding our country's spiritual, emotional, and moral values, and people looked to the church because they wanted to hear from God. As a result of this crisis, many people's hearts were softened, leaving them open to hearing and receiving the good news of Jesus Christ. God used (and continues to use) the church to connect to a lost world that desperately needs Him.

Paul's difficult circumstances represented no international crisis, but God still used them to minister to those around the world, most notably in Rome. Read Philippians 1:12–14. What happened as a result of Paul's circumstances?

_____

_____

_____

_____

Cheer Number Two: The Church's Significance in the Community

The church in the world begins with the church in the community, and what an assortment of churches we see! From traditional to non-traditional and fundamental to liberal, the church contains a wide variety of denominations and an even broader range of non-denominational assemblies. But a variety of motives can exist even within a single church or a ministry.

Take a few moments to read Philippians 1:15–18. What was Paul's main message in these verses?

_____

_____

_____

_____

Out of selfishness, Paul's opponents preached Christ to spite Paul while he stayed in prison. But Paul still rejoiced because Christ was proclaimed. Even today, people's motives for preaching the gospel are not always pure. But, according to Paul, all that matters is that the gospel is preached. When people are hearing the message of salvation through Jesus Christ, their lives will be transformed. And their communities will be transformed, as well.

U.S.News & World Report revealed that the local church provides the strongest influence in bringing isolated individuals to a community event. More people regularly come to church than to any other cultural or voluntary organization in America.[5] Clearly, we as the church must be doing something right!

Cheer Number Three: The Church's Significance in the Christian

We have already seen a number of blessings that are experienced by believers involved in a local church. Paul described a few more benefits in Philippians 1:27–30. Read these verses.

In what manner should we conduct ourselves as believers? Why?

_____

_____

_____

_____

Christians need the local church! Those who become disillusioned or lose faith in the church and walk away tend to struggle in one or more of the four areas listed below. Read verses 27–30 again and note where each of the four areas appears.

1. *Accountability*—being transparent with others.
   (Verse:_____)

2. *Consistency*—remaining faithful in one's walk with Christ.
   (Verse:_____)

3. *Unity*—seeking oneness as opposed to independence.
   (Verse:_____)

4. *Stability*—holding steady when the pressures of life hit.
   (Verse:_____)

In which one (or more) of these four areas could you improve?

_____

_____

_____

In what specific ways can your friends, family members, or small-group members encourage you as you seek to grow in these areas?

_____

_____

_____

THE CHURCH'S ORDINANCES: THE RITE STUFF

The church's contribution to the world, the community, and the life of the Christian is signified by its ordinances. The Lord Jesus gave believers two ordinances to follow. The first, baptism, is biblically understood as a one-time event that takes place at the beginning of the Christian life, after a person has accepted Christ. The second ordinance, the Lord's Supper, takes place repeatedly throughout the life of a believer.

Water Baptism

Let's read what both Jesus and Paul had to say about baptism. At first glance, they actually seem to contradict each other! First, look at Jesus's Great Commission in Matthew 28:19–20:

> Go therefore and make disciples of all the nations, baptizing
> them in the name of the Father and the Son and the Holy
> Spirit, teaching them to observe all that I commanded you; and
> lo, I am with you always, even to the end of the age.

Now, read Paul's words in 1 Corinthians 1:17:

> For Christ did not send me to baptize, but to preach the gospel—not with words of human wisdom, lest the cross of Christ be emptied of its power. (NIV)

What do you think Paul meant when he said, "Christ did not send me to baptize," when you read that Jesus clearly commanded baptism in the Great Commission?

_____

_____

_____

_____

 How does Paul's statement help us to appreciate the Great Commission?

_____

_____

_____

Getting to the Root

In most instances where the New Testament uses the Greek verb *baptidzo*, our English Bibles translate it "baptize." In English, the word *baptize* almost always has one meaning: the ritual use of water. But the Greek word has a broader meaning. For example, outside the New Testament, *baptidzo* was frequently used to refer to a piece of fabric placed into dye.[6] The word assumed a figurative usage suggesting that when an object was *placed into* something (like dye), it took on the characteristics of, *or became identified with*, the thing it was placed into. So, in addition to its literal usage, baptism took on the additional meaning of *identification*. This figurative use of *baptidzo* was just as common as the literal usage.

John the Baptist used both the literal and figurative senses of the word when he said, "I baptize you with water, but He will baptize you with the Holy Spirit" (Mark 1:8). Jesus commanded literal baptism as a way for believers to demonstrate outwardly that they chose to *identify with Him* as His disciples (see Matthew 28:19–20).

In Case You Were Wondering

Q: I recently attended a church where the pastor taught that a person must be baptized by immersion before he or she can be truly saved. Is this true? What does the Bible say?

A: If we say that a person has to be baptized to be saved, we are adding something to the *only* prerequisite the Bible requires of a person for salvation: *faith*. The apostle Paul used Abraham as the leading example of one who was saved by grace *through faith alone*—before the rite of circumcision, before the Old Testament Law (see Romans 4:9–13).

More specifically, the New Testament teaches the ordinance of "believer's baptism." One who *has believed* in Christ may be baptized to signify his or her faith (see Acts 10:47; 11:16–17; 19:1–5). In every biblical context where water baptism is mentioned along with belief, faith always precedes the ordinance of baptism (see 1 Peter 3:21).

In biblical contexts where baptism is included in the proclamation of the gospel, the inclusion of the ordinance of baptism only indicates a public transfer of allegiance to Christ. For example, Peter's command in Acts 2:38, "be baptized in the name of Jesus Christ for the forgiveness of your sins," is often misapplied in the church today. Peter gave the sermon in a context of Jews who would have understood baptism as a *proof* of faith—not a *part* of faith. Most of us in America have no qualms about being baptized in public. But in many other countries today, the meaning of water baptism is much more similar to what it was in Acts 2 — a testimony to the community and to the world. It represents a complete break from the past. And it is common for newly baptized Christians in other countries to be arrested, spend time in jail, lose their family, or even lose their lives for the sake of the gospel.

The Lord's Supper

Unlike baptism, which occurs once at the beginning of a Christian's life, the Lord's Supper takes place numerous times throughout the life of a believer. This makes sense because baptism pictures *conversion*, while the Lord's Supper represents *communion* with God.

Interestingly, the first Lord's Supper occurred at what we usually call the "Last Supper," referring to Jesus's last meal with His disciples before His death. Writing to the Corinthians, the apostle Paul brings us back to that significant event:

> For I received from the Lord that which I also delivered to you, that the Lord Jesus in the night in which He was betrayed took bread; and when He had given thanks, He broke it and said, "This is My body, which is for you; do this in remembrance of Me." (1 Corinthians 11:23–24)

Jesus didn't mean that the bread *was* His physical body; the broken bread *represented* His broken body. The wine also *represents* the blood of Christ. We don't consume the literal body and blood of Jesus, which would imply that the Lord's Supper involves Christ resacrificing Himself over and over again for our sins. Peter wrote, "Christ also died for sins, *once for all* . . . " (1 Peter 3:18, emphasis added). The book of Hebrews emphasizes repeatedly that we no longer need to provide sacrifices for our sins. Christ's solitary sacrifice remains sufficient.

Which of Jesus's commands does Paul quote in 1 Corinthians 11:24? Why would Jesus say this?

_____

_____

_____

_____

Digging Deeper

The Peace Offering

In the Old Testament, believers took part in a number of offerings which represented different aspects of their relationship with God. The peace offering provided an opportunity to commemorate the fact that a believer had *peace and fellowship* with God (Leviticus 3; 7:15–16, 31–32). The worshipper would offer an animal for sacrifice, and he or she would share the parts of the animal with other worshippers and the attending priests in the tabernacle.

This peace offering, also called a fellowship offering, closely depicted what we celebrate in the Lord's Supper. "Take, eat:" Jesus said, "this is my body" (see 1 Corinthians 11:24 KJV). Like the Jews in the tabernacle, we partake of one body—one sacrifice—not in order to make peace with God, but to commemorate that we already have peace, fellowship, and communion with the Lord.

Peace, fellowship, worship, and communion. Are you helping the church (both locally and worldwide) to achieve these vital goals? If not, what needs to change so you can give three heartfelt cheers for the church?

THE FAMILY OF GOD

21

ENCOURAGEMENT SERVED FAMILY STYLE
Selected Scriptures

One *Far Side* cartoon shows a group of cowboys around a campfire at night. All eyes turn to stare at one cowhand as another announces, "Hey, everyone! Simmons here just uttered a discouraging word!"[1] If we could add an additional frame, we'd probably see Simmons lying flat on his back, boots in the air, with a single wisp of smoke rising from his chest.

Whether we're home on the range or working at the office, none of us likes a discourager. Rather than offering solutions, these naysayers shovel out all the reasons why something won't work, how someone did something badly, or why everybody's wrong but them. Emotionally, these people tend to add weight to your load and toss a wet blanket over your feelings of joy.

We might expect such grumblings from disgruntled colleagues or neighbors. But what can you do when these critics sit beside you in church, worshiping the same God as you, bringing discouraging words with them? We can find a biblical solution by examining the pages of Scripture, where we find a command to *encourage one another*.

ENCOURAGEMENT EXPLAINED

We will discuss biblical encouragement in more detail, but first, let's explore the opposite of encouragement: *discouragement*. In his signature style, Garrison Keillor wrote about the Lake Wobegon Schroeders, so named because nine of the baseball team's members were the sons of E. J. Schroeder. Keillor illustrated this father's discouraging demeanor in the following story:

> His sons could never please him, and if they did, he forgot
> about it. Once, against Freeport, his oldest boy, Edwin Jim, Jr.,
> turned and ran to the centerfield fence for a long, long, long fly

ball. He threw his glove forty feet in the air to snag the ball and caught the ball and glove. When he turned toward the dugout to see if his dad had seen it, E. J. was on his feet clapping, but when he saw the boy look to him, he immediately pretended he was swatting mosquitoes. The batter was called out, the third out. Jim ran back to the bench and stood by his dad. E. J. sat chewing in silence and finally said, "I saw a man in Superior, Wisconsin, do that a long time ago. But he did it at night, and the ball was hit a lot harder."[2]

Merriam-Webster's Dictionary defines the word *discourage* as follows: "to deprive of courage or confidence; to dishearten; to hinder by disfavoring; to attempt to dissuade."[3]

Think of someone you know who fits this definition of a "discourager." (But don't write down his or her name!) How do this person's discouraging words, actions, or attitudes make you feel?

_____

_____

_____

_____

We've all felt the pain of discouragement, haven't we? Rather than being discouragers, we want to be *encouragers*. We want to be people with positive attitudes who bring joy to others and help them reach their full potential in Christ.

We've all been touched by friends and family members who have encouraged us by believing in us and seeing the best in us. These people have been powerful motivating forces in our lives. And we want to be the same for them as well as for each person with whom we interact each day.

Scott Adams, the creator of the popular "Dilbert" cartoon, revealed how one person's encouragement completely changed his career as a cartoonist:

When I was trying to become a syndicated cartoonist, I sent my portfolio to one cartoon editor after another—and received one rejection after another. One editor even called to suggest that I take art classes. Then Sarah Gillespie, an editor at United

Media and one of the real experts in the field, called to offer me a contract. At first, I didn't believe her. I asked if I'd have to change my style, get a partner—or learn how to draw. But she believed I was already good enough to be a nationally syndicated cartoonist.

Her confidence in me completely changed my frame of reference: it altered how I thought about my own abilities. This may sound bizarre, but from the minute I got off the phone with her, I could draw better. You can see a marked improvement in the quality of the cartoons I drew after that conversation.[4]

The dictionary defines *encourage* as "to inspire with hope, courage, or confidence; hearten; to give support to; foster; to stimulate; spur."[5]

Think of someone you know who fits this definition of an encourager. After writing down his or her name, describe in one sentence how this person's words, actions, and attitudes make you feel.

_____

_____

_____

_____

Why is encouragement so important in your life?

_____

_____

_____

_____

Undoubtedly, we all need frequent, refreshing drinks from the spring of encouragement. Without uplifting words from others, we can become discouraged and feel like quitting. So it makes sense that the Lord would *command* us to encourage one another. If we can't find encouragement among fellow Christians, where else can we look?

THE BIBLICAL BASIS FOR ENCOURAGEMENT

The book of Hebrews is intended to help us see Christ as He really is. Jesus, the God-Man, ranks superior in every way to all the Old Testament priests, prophets, kings, and sacrifices. He fulfills the reality of God's promises, while all others served as a shadow or "type" of the Messiah who was to come.

Read aloud the following passage from the book of Hebrews:

> Therefore, brethren, since we have confidence to enter the holy place by the blood of Jesus, by a new and living way which He inaugurated for us through the veil, that is, His flesh, and since we have a great priest over the house of God, let us draw near with a sincere heart in full assurance of faith, having our hearts sprinkled clean from an evil conscience and our bodies washed with pure water. Let us hold fast the confession of our hope without wavering, for He who promised is faithful; and let us consider how to stimulate one another to love and good deeds. (10:19–24)

In verses 19–21, the author reminds us that we enjoy a relationship with God the Father in which we can enter His very presence. Christ has made this fellowship possible by bridging the gap between us and God—by becoming our final priest and sacrifice. Stemming from this wonderful privilege we have in Christ, the author then issues three commands in three verses. Each command is introduced by the words "Let us . . ." Observe the commands in 10:22–24 and write each one below.

Verse 22: "Let us . . . _____."

Verse 23: "Let us . . . _____."

Verse 24: "Let us . . . _____."

How do these three commands relate to each other? Is there a progression? If so, what is it?

_____

_____

_____

_____

Getting to the Root

The word *stimulate* in Hebrews 10:25 comes from the Greek word *paroxusmos*. The word occurs elsewhere in the New Testament in the context of provoking a sharp disagreement (see Acts 15:39). Similarly, the Septuagint (the Greek translation of the Old Testament) uses the word twice in reference to God's strong anger (see Deuteronomy 29:28; Jeremiah 32:37). The unusual usage of *paroxusmos* in Hebrews reflects not an irritation to anger, but a strong motivation, provoking, or spurring on to love and good deeds. The word suggests that we should consider how to encourage life-change in others, producing in them dissatisfaction with anything less than practical godliness.[6]

Entering God's holy presence, persevering in solid doctrine, and encouraging one another to love and good deeds are not three separate "majors" in the college of Christianity. Each command ultimately finds its obedience in the balance of all the others. Can we exclusively devote ourselves to entering God's presence apart from true doctrine? Or can we devote ourselves to doctrine apart from God or people?

The author of Hebrews continues in 10:25 by explaining *how* we can stimulate one another to love and good deeds:

> Not forsaking our own assembling together, as is the habit of some, but encouraging one another; and all the more as you see the day drawing near.

There's our word — "Not forsaking . . . but *encouraging* one another." This command has been issued to every Christian, not just a few. We can't stimulate others to love and good deeds if we're not around them! We can't be an encouragement if we live our lives like hermits hiding in caves, pushing people away from us. People who are out of touch with reality won't be well equipped to encourage others. Encouragement is a face-to-face endeavor.

It's easy for us, as Christians, to become attracted to theological study to the exclusion of building close relationships with each other. But we need both! The church, a place that provides strong spiritual instruction, should also be a place that offers deep fellowship and personal compassion. The same

Scriptures that encourage us to grow in knowledge also exhort us to grow in love, grace, and acceptance of others. The passages that urge clear thinking and wise discernment are well-balanced by other passages that affirm our call to understand and encourage one another.

List at least four benefits you have personally experienced from regularly attending church and experiencing fellowship with other believers.

_____

_____

_____

_____

ENCOURAGEMENT: HOW TO DO IT

Because our words are our primary means of offering encouragement to others, let's allow God's Word to have its way with that little instrument that produces words: the tongue. Several Bible books describe the power of the tongue, but we'll limit our study to the wise book of Proverbs.

Look up each of these Proverbs and note what they teach about our words.

Proverbs 10:11–13

_____

_____

_____

_____

Proverbs 10:19–21

_____

_____

_____

Proverbs 12:17–18

_____

_____

_____

_____

Can you remember a time when you felt depressed, hurting, or hopeless, and someone spoke words of life to you? Maybe you remember being hurt so deeply that your emotional wound took a long time to heal. And just about the time it started to heal, someone opened the wound again. Hopefully, in the midst of your pain and emotional fog, someone in God's family cared enough to look you in the eye and speak words of grace and comfort to you — saying just the right thing at just the right time. "The tongue of the wise brings healing." That's the kind of words we want to have — words that encourage and heal. Mark Twain once said, "I can live for two months on a good compliment." [7]

But before we let our tongues out of the house, let's deal with them there — in our homes. If walls could talk, they would reveal that when we're at home, our words and actions expose our "true colors." Our words bring either life or death to those we love. Consider one more proverb, but think of it in the context of your own family:

> Death and life are in the power of the tongue,
> And those who love it will eat its fruit. (Proverbs 18:21)

One father told his son, who had just graduated from college with a music degree, "So, what are you going to do now? Get a job mowing yards?" In other words, "Your degree is worthless." And the son took to heart the painful message, "You're worthless." *Death* is in the power of the tongue. But wait — so is *life*!

Consider the example of Benjamin West, who loved to paint as a youngster. One day, he painted a picture but splattered oil paint everywhere, making a huge mess! He tried to clean it up before his mother came home, but she walked in and saw it all. She walked over to the painting, looked at it, and said, "My, what a beautiful painting of your sister." Then she kissed his cheek and left. West later said that with that kiss, he became a painter. [8]

Our words of encouragement will not be overlooked or easily erased. Even today, each of us can remember life-changing words spoken by a parent, a teacher, a coach, a pastor, or a friend. Words have power—for death or for life. We can't change yesterday, but just think about the possibilities that await us tomorrow! It's never too late for us to start doing what is right. Let your words put "skin" on Scripture, and start encouraging one another.

 ## In Case You Were Wondering

Q: Who am I responsible to encourage?

A: Ideally, we should try to speak words of life to everyone we meet. But let your commitment to encourage begin at home and then expand outward to include all people within your sphere of influence. Don't think that just because you have close relationships with those in your own family, encouragement will automatically happen in your home. Often, those closest to us hear our kind words the least often. But that can (and should) change! Make a commitment today to genuinely encourage each person you meet, including those under your own roof. On the list below, place a check next to each person after you have encouraged him or her.

____ Your spouse

____ Your child(ren)

____ Your parent(s)

____ Your roommate or close friend

Then venture outside your walls and encourage your pastor and church workers, your supervisor or colleagues at work, and those who recently may have heard discouraging words from you. Watch and see how encouraging words from your tongue can bring life!

A CLASSIC EXAMPLE OF AN ENCOURAGER

The Bible abounds with examples of encouragers. Caleb, Ruth, Nehemiah, Barnabas (whose name even means "Son of Encouragement"), and of course, Jesus Himself all spoke words of life to those who needed to hear it.

David's life offers one of the finest examples of words that healed during a discouraging time. Remember the immediate fame he achieved after killing Goliath? David went from being a nobody to becoming a national hero overnight, and the people sang his praises: "Saul has slain his thousands, and David his ten thousands!" Everybody sang along, except for one person — King Saul. Everybody applauded except the one who wanted all the applause for himself. Saul's jealousy and fits of rage forced David to live on the run as a fugitive for twelve years. The Psalms record some of David's most heart-wrenching cries to God during these years of fear and dependence.

Ironically, Saul's son Jonathan, of all people, developed a close relationship with David. They loved each other as best friends (see 1 Samuel 18:3). Once, when a desperate David lay hidden in the wilderness, Jonathan offered these healing words:

> And Jonathan, Saul's son, arose and went to David at Horesh, and encouraged him in God. Thus he said to him, "Do not be afraid, because the hand of Saul my father will not find you, and you will be king over Israel and I will be next to you; and Saul my father knows that also." (1 Samuel 23:16–17)

Which three verbs are used in 23:16? Write them here.

_____ _____ _____

Note the intent behind Jonathan's actions. His *purpose* was to encourage David. Now notice *how* he did it. Read 1 Samuel 16:12–13 for some background on the story. Now, from 23:17 above, how did Jonathan encourage David "in God"?

_____

_____

_____

_____

Later David faced desperation again—and this time, he was alone, without Jonathan to come to his aid. Read 1 Samuel 30:6 and note David's response as he stood all alone.

_____

_____

_____

_____

Thinking about *how* Jonathan encouraged David, what value do you see in reminding people of God's promises? What specific passages could you take to someone who is struggling with discouragement?

_____

_____

_____

What can you do the next time you face discouragement? To whom might you turn?

_____

_____

_____

_____

Digging Deeper

Flattery Gets Us Nowhere

Benjamin Franklin said, "The same man cannot be both friend and flatterer."[9] As we encourage others, we must carefully differentiate between encouragement and flattery. *Merriam-Webster's Collegiate Dictionary* defines *flattery* as "insincere or excessive praise."[10] Even if we speak accurately, we're still guilty of flattery if self-interest motivates our words (see Proverbs 7:21; 1 Thessalonians 2:3–5). Ultimately, honeyed words spoken with ulterior motives cause only harm in the end. Proverbs 29:5 reminds us that "a man who flatters his neighbor is spreading a net for his steps."

True, biblical encouragement will flow naturally from a heart that has experienced the love, peace, joy, and grace of Christ. Rather than resorting to vague pleasantries, empty compliments, or false flattery, seek to provide *real encouragement* to those around you today. An uplifting phone call, a thoughtful card, a small gift, and even just a few kind words can mean so much to a person in need of encouragement. In fact, the words you speak today may have an eternal effect on the life of someone else. So start encouraging!

22

Worship: Let It Shine! Let It Shine!

Psalm 95:1–5

The opening act of any big-name concert provides an up-and-coming artist or group the opportunity to warm up a crowd who really came to hear someone else. It also allows a buffer for all the latecomers to find their seat and for the sound technicians to tweak the system. Everybody knows the *real* concert begins about a half-hour after it starts, so the audience tolerates the opening act like they would a television commercial. They think, "This will be over soon, and the real reason I'm here will begin." In short, the opener compares little to the headliner, and if the opening act were the only show, everybody would stay home.

Interestingly, we often bring with us the same mindset to church that we take to a concert. Read the opening paragraph as it is reworded below. Here, we've substituted the worship portion of a service for the "opening act," and the preacher's message replaces the term "headliner."

The opening activity of any church service provides a worship leader or worship team the opportunity to warm up a congregation who really came to hear someone else. It also allows a buffer for all the latecomers to find their seat and for the sound technicians to tweak the system. Everybody knows the *real* ministry begins about a half-hour after the service starts, so the congregation tolerates the worship like they would a television commercial. They think, "This will be over soon, and the real reason I'm here will begin." In short, the worship portion compares little to the preaching, and if worship were the only activity, everybody would stay home.

It's an uncomfortable comparison, isn't it? And yet this scenario plays itself out every single Sunday in many evangelical churches across the nation. This seems to happen especially in churches where the pastor's teaching gift is widely appreciated. Statistically speaking, for many individuals in church, and for most senior pastors, worship takes a back seat to the message. George Barna's research has shown that only one out of every four pastors identified worship as one of the top priorities in their church. Nearly two-thirds of regular attendees say they have never experienced God's presence at a church service, and almost half have not experienced God's presence in church over a given year.[1] A. W. Tozer said, "Worship acceptable to God is the missing crown jewel in evangelical Christianity."[2] Let's see if we can find this missing jewel!

THE MISSING JEWEL DISCOVERED

First of all, what thoughts or images come to your mind when you hear the word *worship*?

_____

_____

_____

_____

Some people think worship means attending church; some imagine listening to a sermon; most think of singing songs, listening to the choir, and enjoying the music played by the church musicians. Even church leadership and churchgoers do not seem to agree on a single understanding of *worship*. It is interesting to note that 47% of all churchgoers understand worship as an activity undertaken for their personal benefit, while most pastors describe the purpose of worship as "connecting with God" (41%) or "experiencing His presence" (30%).[3]

So how can we rediscover the "missing jewel" of worship? How can we understand the facets of worship and then turn the word from a noun into a verb by living it out? How can we make worship practical and not just theoretical?

THE IDENTITY AND MEANING OF WORSHIP

Psalm 95 introduces us to God's understanding of worship. From the earliest days of the church, believers turned to this psalm as both a motivation and a guide for worship.[4] Let's allow the Spirit of God to train us regarding what worship means and how the Lord intends for us to carry it out.

Think about the last time you went to church. What attitude did you bring with you as you entered? Frustration from trying to get your family ready and out the door on time? Anger over a family squabble? Irritation because someone else sat in "your" seat? Hopefully, in the best-case scenario, you were able to set aside all of these distractions and enter God's presence with a worshipful attitude.

Now, read the first two verses of Psalm 95. The psalmist offers the opening verses as an invitation to enter God's presence. Picture entering into *God's presence* for a moment. Not simply entering a temple — or for us, a church building — but worshipfully and solemnly entering into the very presence of God. We come with a purpose.

What three actions do these verses say we should do? (Each begins with the challenge: "Let us . . .")

_____

_____

_____

_____

What attitudes do these verses say we should bring into God's presence?

_____

_____

_____

_____

Do you tend to rely on the church's atmosphere to provide you with a worshipful attitude, or do you choose a worshipful heart regardless of your surroundings? What attitudes or acts help you to prepare your heart and mind for worship?

_____

_____

_____

_____

The text provides a clear reason to enter God's presence. Read
Psalm 95:3–5. Why do we come before our God with thanksgiving and
joyful shouts?

_____

_____

_____

_____

The text does not force worship on us but provides the reason that our
worship cannot be contained: "The Lord is a great God . . . above all gods."
God's greatness reveals itself in objective ways that we can clearly see—from
the greatest heights of the earth to the depths of the ocean—and everything
in between. God holds all things in His hands; His hands formed them all.

**Now, read verses 6 and 7. Which terms in these verses illustrate what our
posture and attitude should be when we come before God in worship?**

_____

_____

_____

_____

 ## Getting to the Root

Our English word *worship* comes from the Old English word
weorthscipe, or "worth-ship,"[5] which indicated an expression of reverence to God because He is *worthy* of praise. But the biblical words
have a more specific meaning. The Hebrew word for *worship* used in
Psalm 95:6, *chawah*, originally meant "to bow in worship; to prostrate oneself."[6] The New Testament Greek word *proskyneō* also refers
to bowing or kneeling as an act of reverence.[7] Early believers went
beyond simply giving God honor by worshiping Him in a prostrate
position of submission and respect, with hearts full of obedience.

To understand how ancient believers worshiped God, try this activity, either by yourself or in your small group. Kneel down, place the palms of your hands on the ground, touch your forehead to the ground, and pray silently for a few moments. How does this position attune you to what the attitude of your heart should be when worshiping God?

_____

_____

_____

_____

Psalm 95:6 not only depicts our *action* before God, it also describes what our *attitude* should be: "worship . . . bow down . . . kneel . . ." A heart that's willing to worship God is a heart that's willing to submit to Him. And so the psalmist challenges believers to allow their worship to run its logical course. Worship ultimately expresses itself in obedience, not simply in joyful singing. Read the rest of the psalm (95:7–11), remembering it in the context of worship.

Did you catch the change of voice from "you" and "your" in verses 7–8 to "Me," "My," and "I" in verses 9–12? The psalmist alerts the readers in verse 7 to listen for God's voice, and then he quotes God's voice directly.

What does God want readers to see through these changes?

_____

_____

_____

_____

This passage refers to specific events in Israel's history that mark times when the Jews deliberately ignored the voice of God. *Meribah* and *Massah* were the dual names of a place that Moses named because of the disobedience that took place there, including his own. *Meribah* means "test" in Hebrew, and *Massah* means "quarrel." At that location, the Israelite people failed to take

God at His Word and enter the Promised Land, and Moses failed to honor God's Word; he struck a rock to bring forth water rather than simply speaking to it as God had commanded (see Numbers 20:1–12). The Israelite people had heard God's Word, but they refused to take it seriously. And so God let them wander in the wilderness for forty long, dusty, exhausting years, and that disobedient generation never entered the Promised Land.

THE SIGNIFICANCE AND PURPOSE OF WORSHIP

Remembering the truth we've learned in Psalm 95, respond briefly to each of the following statements that identify the significance and purpose of worship.

Worship magnifies my God and eclipses my fears.

_____

_____

_____

_____

Worship enlarges my horizons and changes my perspective.

_____

_____

_____

_____

Worship refreshes my spirit and enhances my work.

_____

_____

_____

_____

The New Testament book of Hebrews applies the timeless truths of Psalm 95 to the Christian life. Derek Kidner notes:

> Hebrews 4:1–13 argues that the psalm still offers us, by its emphatic *Today*, a rest beyond anything that Joshua won, namely a share in God's own Sabbath rest: enjoyment of His finished work not merely of creation but of redemption. . . . If this psalm is about worship, it could give no blunter indication that the heart of the matter is severely practical.[8]

Some Often Overlooked Facets of the Jewel

We can cultivate a greater love for worship by examining some facets of the jewel of worship that are often overlooked. The first makes a practical connection between worship and obedience.

Worship Is Needed in the Present

Worship is not merely something that the ancients did in the past, nor is it simply part of a Sunday service we attend. A life of worship is a lifestyle of honor, service, and praise we offer to God. Paul exhorts us in Romans 12:1:

> I urge you therefore, brethren, by the mercies of God, to present your bodies a living and holy sacrifice, which is your spiritual service of worship.

What does it mean for us to offer our bodies as living and holy sacrifices? How does the presenting of our bodies as living sacrifices relate to worship?

_____

_____

_____

_____

Can we sacrifice our bodies apart from sacrificing our hearts and minds? How would we go about offering up our hearts and minds to God?

_____

_____

_____

_____

Worship remains, in essence, an offering of our lives to God in response to His perfect character. Just as Psalm 95 calls us to worship because of the *greatness* of our God, so Romans 12:1 calls us to worship because of the *mercy* of God. Both passages intimately link worship with the personal application of God's Word.

We worship God when we sacrifice our own selfish desires to accomplish His perfect desires. Listen to the practical outworking of becoming a living sacrifice in the verses that follow:

> For through the grace given to me I say to everyone among you not to think more highly of himself than he ought to think; . . . Be of the same mind toward one another; do not be haughty in mind, but associate with the lowly. Do not be wise in your own estimation. (Romans 12:3, 16)

 ## In Case You Were Wondering

Q: Our church has experienced a great deal of division with regard to worship styles. The older members prefer traditional music and hymns, while the younger members prefer more upbeat, contemporary music and praise choruses. Does Scripture address worship styles? If not, how should we go about reconciling these differences?

A: All too often, worship in the church becomes a source of division rather than the means of unity that God intended. When we refuse to worship because, for example, the church plays a style of music we don't prefer, we resemble the Pharisees who took offense at Jesus because He didn't follow their rules and traditions (Mark 7:5–8). Worship in the church is not simply individual, but *corporate*. We're the body of Christ, and we as believers are not unified by our common *tastes*, but by our common *faith*.

Our ability to worship God with joy should not hinge on our musical preferences. Our worship is a response to the greatness of God and the mercy of God. Worship *can be* uplifting, entertaining, and personally nourishing—but these are byproducts of a grateful heart that worships regardless of the environment. The Bible calls worship a "sacrifice of praise" (Hebrews 13:15). Praise is a *sacrifice* we give to God—not something a church offers to us. We may be called to sacrifice our own preferences to serve others, but we're still called to praise God with a worshipful heart.

Think for a moment about what you can contribute to your church's worship service to bring unity rather than division. Write your response below.

_____

_____

_____

_____

Worship Is Sought by God

Only one place in the entire Bible says that God seeks something from us: God seeks *worshipers!* In chapter 9 of this workbook, we spent significant time studying the fourth chapter of the book of John. Read once again what Jesus spoke to the woman at the well:

> "You worship what you do not know; we worship what we know, for salvation is from the Jews. But an hour is coming, and now is, when the true worshipers will worship the Father in spirit and truth; *for such people the Father seeks to be His worshipers.*" (John 4:22–23, emphasis added)

What two essential ingredients of worship does Jesus mention?

_____

_____

_____

_____

Our worship *must* remain in truth—in keeping with the revealed Word of God. But it is important to notice that we don't just bring truth to worship; we also bring a prepared heart. Jesus said we worship in *spirit* as well as in truth. Jesus mentioned this because the nature of God is spirit (not flesh); when we worship Him, our spirits must be engaged. We must involve the immaterial part of us that makes up the human spirit, heart, soul, and mind. And in order to present our bodies as living sacrifices, we must keep God's greatness and mercy always in the forefront of our thoughts. Having grateful hearts makes us true worshipers—those who aren't just going through the motions or stirring up emotions, but offering our lives to God. God seeks worshipers like this.

Digging Deeper

The Priesthood of the Believer

In the Old Testament, God offered strict commands to the Levites who served as priests. High priests could marry only women who were virgins: "And he shall take a wife in her virginity" (Leviticus 21:13), and they could not touch a dead body except for that of a close relative (Leviticus 21:1). These commands regulated not only the professional duties of a priest, but his private life, as well.

The apostle Peter applied the timeless truths of the priesthood to all believers: "[You] are being built up as a spiritual house for a holy priesthood, to *offer up spiritual sacrifices* acceptable to God through Jesus Christ" (1 Peter 2:5, emphasis added). Peter revealed the purpose of Israel's priests as true of believers in Jesus Christ.

However, just because Peter calls our actions "*spiritual* sacrifices" doesn't mean they're not *real* sacrifices. These sacrifices include offering our bodies as "living sacrifices" (Romans 12:1), our financial gifts as "a fragrant offering" (Philippians 4:18 NIV), our vocal worship as "a sacrifice of praise" (Hebrews 13:15), and even the conversion of unbelievers as "an offering acceptable to God" (Romans 15:16). Every Christian, as part of a holy priesthood, is called to make these sacrifices.

> The marrying and burying laws for the priests revealed that their roles extended beyond the tabernacle to their entire lives. As a holy priesthood, we, too, carry our spiritual lives home with us, to work with us, to the movies with us, and to church with us. We're called to dedicate every part of our lives to God—what we do, how we act, whom we choose to marry, where we choose to work, and a thousand smaller daily decisions. Like the priests of old, we should demonstrate consistency rather than a division between our "spiritual" and "secular" lives.

THE SPARKLING BEAUTY OF THE REDISCOVERED JEWEL

Worship represents far more than a warm-up to hearing the Word of God. Worship *is* the Word of God, applied every moment of every day. *Our lives should be the ultimate, unending worship service.* Our Monday-through-Friday worship (and even our Saturday-night worship) remains as critical to God as our Sunday-morning worship. Convicting, isn't it?

What a change of heart can take place when we realize that our Sunday-morning worship is just an extension of the worship we have offered God all week! We come together on Sundays to offer God corporately what we have already offered Him privately. We bring Him our sacrifice of praise—in awe of His greatness and in response to His glorious mercy. Now, take your jewel of worship and let it shine!

How to Begin a Relationship with God

Growing deep in the Christian life involves examining our spiritual roots. It means that we must take a good, honest look at ourselves and the spiritual state of our lives. Our spiritual journey must begin with God, the Lord of the universe, who knows us better than we know ourselves. He has complete sovereignty over our lives, but we must choose to follow Him.

If God is the source and center of our lives, how can we come to know Him? How can we be sure that we are in a right relationship with the only One who knows the end from the beginning and can direct us in the way we should go?

The most marvelous book in the world, the Bible, marks the path to God with four vital truths. Let's look at each marker in detail.

Our Spiritual Condition: Totally Depraved

The first truth is rather personal. One look in the mirror of Scripture, and our human condition becomes painfully clear:

> There is none righteous, not even one;
> There is none who understands,
> There is none who seeks for God;
> All have turned aside, together they have become useless;
> There is none who does good,
> There is not even one. (Romans 3:10–12)

We are all sinners through and through—totally depraved. Now, that doesn't mean we've committed every atrocity known to humankind. We're not as *bad* as we can be, just as *bad off* as we can be. Sin colors all our thoughts, motives, words, and actions.

You still don't believe it? Look around. Everything around us bears the marks of our sinful nature. Despite our best efforts to create a perfect world, crime statistics continue to soar, divorce rates keep climbing, and families keep crumbling.

Something has gone terribly wrong in our society and within ourselves — something deadly. Contrary to how the world would repackage it, "me-first" living doesn't equal rugged individuality and freedom; it equals death. Paul wrote in his letter to the Romans, "The wages of sin is death" (Romans 6:23) — emotional and physical death through sin's destructiveness and spiritual death from God's righteous judgment of our sin. This brings us to the second marker: God's character.

GOD'S CHARACTER: INFINITELY HOLY

Solomon observed the condition of the world and the people in it and concluded, "Vanity of vanities; all is vanity" (Ecclesiastes 1:2; 12:8). The fact that we know things are not as they should be points us to a standard of goodness and righteousness beyond ourselves. Our sense of injustice in life on earth implies a perfect standard of justice elsewhere. That standard and source is God Himself. And God's standard of holiness contrasts starkly with our sinful condition.

Scripture reminds us that "God is light, and in Him there is no darkness at all" (1 John 1:5). He is absolutely holy — which creates a problem for us. If He is so pure, how can we who are so impure relate to Him?

Perhaps we could try being better people, and therefore, we might tip the scales in favor of our good deeds. We could seek out greater wisdom and knowledge for self-improvement. Throughout history, people have attempted to live up to God's standard by keeping the Ten Commandments or living by their own code of ethics. Unfortunately, however, no one can come close to satisfying the demands of God's law in his or her own strength.

OUR NEED: A SUBSTITUTE

So here we are, sinners by nature, sinners by choice, trying to pull ourselves up by our own bootstraps and attain a relationship with our holy Creator. (By the way, have you ever seen anyone actually try to pull himself up by his bootstraps? Guess what? It's *impossible*.) Every time we try to achieve righteousness by our own merit, we fall flat on our faces. We can't live a good enough life to make up for our sin, because God's standard isn't just "good enough"— it's perfection. And we can't make amends for the offense our sin has created without dying for it.

Who can get us out of this mess?

If someone could live perfectly, honoring God's law, and could bear sin's death penalty for us—in our place—then we would be saved from our predicament. But is there such a person? Thankfully, yes!

Meet your substitute—*Jesus Christ*. He's the One who took death's place for you so that you could be reconciled to God and have eternal life! The apostle Paul wrote:

> [God] made [Jesus Christ] who knew no sin to be sin on our behalf, so that we might become the righteousness of God in Him. (2 Corinthians 5:21)

God's Provision: A Savior

God rescued us by sending His Son, Jesus, to die for our sins on the cross (1 John 4:9–10). Jesus was fully human and fully divine (John 1:1, 18), a truth that ensures His understanding of our weaknesses, His power to forgive, and His ability to bridge the gap between God and us (Romans 5:6–11). In short, we are "justified as a gift by His grace through the redemption which is in Christ Jesus" (Romans 3:24). Two words in this verse bear further explanation: *justified* and *redemption*.

Justification is God's act of mercy in which He *declares* believing sinners righteous, even while they are still in their sinning state. Justification doesn't mean that God *makes* us righteous, so that we never sin again, but rather that He *declares* us righteous—much like a judge could choose to pardon a guilty criminal. Because Jesus took our sin upon Himself and suffered our judgment on the cross, God forgives our debt and proclaims us PARDONED.

Redemption is God's act of paying the ransom price to release us from our bondage to sin. Held hostage by Satan, we were shackled by the heavy chains of sin and death. But, like a loving parent whose child has been kidnapped, desperate to rescue His beloved son or daughter, God willingly paid the ransom for you. And what a price He paid! He gave His only Son to bear your sins—past, present, and future. Jesus's death and resurrection broke your chains and set you free to become a child of God (Romans 6:16–18, 22; Galatians 4:4–7).

PLACING YOUR FAITH IN CHRIST

These four truths describe how God has provided a way to Himself through Jesus Christ. Since the price of our sin has been paid in full by God, we must respond to His free gift of eternal life in total faith and confidence in Him to save us. We must step forward into the relationship with God that He has prepared for us—not by doing good works or being a good person, but by coming to Him just as we are and accepting His justification and redemption by faith. In the book of Ephesians, Paul wrote:

> For by grace you have been saved through faith; and that not of yourselves, it is the gift of God; not as a result of works, so that no one may boast. (Ephesians 2:8–9)

We accept God's gift of salvation simply by placing our faith in Christ alone for the forgiveness of our sins. Would you like to enter a relationship with your Creator by trusting in Christ as your Savior? If so, here's a simple prayer you can use to express your faith:

> *Dear God,*
>
> *I know that my sin has put a barrier between You and me, and I want to confess that sin and ask for Your forgiveness. Thank You for sending Your Son, Jesus, to die in my place. I trust in Jesus alone to forgive my sins, and I accept His gift of eternal life. I ask Jesus to be my personal Savior and the Lord of my life. Thank You.*
>
> *In Jesus's name, Amen.*

If you've prayed this prayer or one like it and you wish to find out more about knowing God and His plan for you, please contact us at Insight for Living. You can speak to one of our pastors on staff by calling or writing to us at the address below.

Of all the spiritual legacies you could leave to those who come after you, none can compare with a life lived by faith in the Son of God, who loved you and gave Himself for you so that you could have eternal life. If you need help growing deeper in the spiritual life, please call or write today.

Insight for Living
Post Office Box 269000
Plano, Texas 75026-9000
1-800-772-8888

Endnotes

Chapter 1

Unless otherwise noted below, all material in this chapter is based on or quoted from "The Value of Knowing the Scoop," a sermon by Charles R. Swindoll, September 29, 1985, and chapter 1 in the *Growing Deep in the Christian Life* companion book.

1. Jaime M. O'Neill, "No Allusions in the Classroom," *Newsweek*, September 23, 1985; 14.

2. Robert L. Thomas, ed., *New American Standard Exhaustive Concordance of the Bible* (Nashville: Holman Bible Publishers, 1981), 1634. Copyright 1981 by The Lockman Foundation. Used by permission. (www.Lockman.org)

Chapter 2

Unless otherwise noted below, all material in this chapter is based on or quoted from "Don't Forget to Add a Cup of Discernment," a sermon by Charles R. Swindoll, September 29, 1985, and chapter 2 in the *Growing Deep in the Christian Life* companion book.

1. Robert L. Thomas, ed., *New American Standard Exhaustive Concordance of the Bible* (Nashville: Holman Bible Publishers, 1981), 1640. Copyright 1981 by The Lockman Foundation. Used by permission. (www.Lockman.org)

2. Thomas, *New American Standard Exhaustive Concordance of the Bible*, 1628.

3. Thomas, *New American Standard Exhaustive Concordance of the Bible*, 1650.

Chapter 3

Unless otherwise noted below, all material in this chapter is based on or quoted from "God's Book — God's Voice," a sermon by Charles R. Swindoll, October 6, 1985, and chapter 3 in the *Growing Deep in the Christian Life* companion book.

1. Robert L. Thomas, ed., *New American Standard Exhaustive Concordance of the Bible* (Nashville: Holman Bible Publishers, 1981), 1640. Copyright 1981 by The Lockman Foundation. Used by permission. (www.Lockman.org)

2. Norman L. Geisler, *Christian Apologetics* (Grand Rapids: Baker Book House, 1997), 376–77.

CHAPTER 4

Unless otherwise noted below, all material in this chapter is based on or quoted from "Handling the Scriptures Accurately," a sermon by Charles R. Swindoll, October 6, 1985, and chapter 4 in the *Growing Deep in the Christian Life* companion book.

1. Robert L. Thomas, ed., *New American Standard Exhaustive Concordance of the Bible* (Nashville: Holman Bible Publishers, 1981), 1584. Copyright 1981 by The Lockman Foundation. Used by permission. (www.Lockman.org)

CHAPTER 5

Unless otherwise noted below, all material in this chapter is based on or quoted from "Knowing God: Life's Major Pursuit," a sermon by Charles R. Swindoll, October 13, 1985, and chapter 5 in the *Growing Deep in the Christian Life* companion book.

1. Robert L. Thomas, ed., *New American Standard Exhaustive Concordance of the Bible* (Nashville: Holman Bible Publishers, 1981), 1605. Copyright 1981 by The Lockman Foundation. Used by permission. (www.Lockman.org)

2. Thomas, *New American Standard Exhaustive Concordance of the Bible*, 1528.

3. C. S. Lewis, *Mere Christianity* (New York: Macmillan Publishing Co., 1960), 118. Copyright © C. S. Lewis Pte. Ltd. 1942, 1943, 1944, 1952. Extract reprinted by permission.

CHAPTER 6

Unless otherwise noted below, all material in this chapter is based on or quoted from "Loving God: Our Ultimate Response," a sermon by Charles R. Swindoll, October 13, 1985, and chapter 6 in the *Growing Deep in the Christian Life* companion book.

1. Robert L. Thomas, ed., *New American Standard Exhaustive Concordance of the Bible* (Nashville: Holman Bible Publishers, 1981), 1486. Copyright 1981 by The Lockman Foundation. Used by permission. (www.Lockman.org)

2. *Merriam-Webster's Collegiate Dictionary*, 10th ed. (Springfield, Mass.: Merriam-Webster, Inc., 2000), see "sovereign."

3. A. W. Tozer, *The Knowledge of the Holy* (San Francisco: HarperSanFrancisco, 1961), 111. Copyright © 1961 by Aiden Wilson Tozer. Reprinted by permission of HarperCollins Publishers.

4. Dr. Jeff Levin, quote accessed at http://www.religionandhealth.com/new2.html. For further information, see Dr. Jeff Levin, *God, Faith, and Health: Exploring the Spirituality-Healing Connection* (New York: John Wiley & Sons, 2001).

CHAPTER 7

Unless otherwise noted below, all material in this chapter is based on or quoted from "Mary's Little Lamb," a sermon by Charles R. Swindoll, December 23, 1973, and chapter 7 in the *Growing Deep in the Christian Life* companion book.

1. See Thomas Edward McComiskey, "Micah," in *The Expositor's Bible Commentary*, vol. 7, ed. Frank E. Gaebelein (Grand Rapids: Zondervan Publishing House, 1985), 427.

CHAPTER 8

Unless otherwise noted below, all material in this chapter is based on or quoted from "When the God-Man Walked Among Us," a sermon by Charles R. Swindoll, October 20, 1985, and chapter 8 in the *Growing Deep in the Christian Life* companion book.

1. John R. W. Stott, *Basic Christianity* (Downers Grove, Ill.: InterVarsity Press, 1958), 21.

2. Frank E. Gaebelein, ed., "Matthew, Mark, Luke" in *The Expositor's Bible Commentary*, vol. 8 (Grand Rapids: Zondervan Publishing House, 1984), 85. With contributors Donald A. Carson, Walter L. Liefeld, and Walter W. Wessel. Copyright © 1984 by The Zondervan Corporation. Used by permission of The Zondervan Corporation.

3. Robert H. Stein, "Jesus Christ," in *The Concise Evangelical Dictionary of Theology*, ed. Walter A. Elwell (Grand Rapids: Baker Book House, 1991), 254.

4. C. S. Lewis, *Mere Christianity* (New York: Macmillan Publishing Co., 1960), 56. Copyright © C. S. Lewis Pte. Ltd. 1942, 1943, 1944, 1952. Extract reprinted by permission.

CHAPTER 9

Unless otherwise noted below, all material in this chapter is based on or quoted from "Changing Lives is Jesus's Business," a sermon by Charles R. Swindoll, October 20, 1985, and chapter 9 in the *Growing Deep in the Christian Life* companion book.

1. Robert L. Thomas, ed., *New American Standard Exhaustive Concordance of the Bible* (Nashville: Holman Bible Publishers, 1981), 1532. Copyright 1981 by The Lockman Foundation. Used by permission. (www.Lockman.org)

2. Michelangelo Buonarroti, quote accessed at http://www.brainyquote.com/quotes/authors/m/michelangelo.html on December 30, 2004.

CHAPTER 10

Unless otherwise noted below, all material in this chapter is based on or quoted from "The Spirit Who Is Not a Ghost," a sermon by Charles R. Swindoll, October 27, 1985, and chapter 10 in the *Growing Deep in the Christian Life* companion book.

1. J. I. Packer, *Keep in Step with the Spirit* (Old Tappan, N.J.: Fleming H. Revell Co., 1984), 57.

2. Robert L. Thomas, ed., *New American Standard Exhaustive Concordance of the Bible* (Nashville: Holman Bible Publishers, 1981), 1595, 1676. Copyright 1981 by The Lockman Foundation. Used by permission. (www.Lockman.org)

3. A. W. Tozer, *The Counselor: Straight Talk about the Holy Spirit from a 20th-Century Prophet* (Camp Hill, Penn.: Christian Publications, Inc., 1993), 41–42. Used by permission of Christian Publications, Inc., 800.233.4443, www.christianpublications.com.

4. Merrill C. Tenney, "The Gospel of John," in *The Expositor's Bible Commentary*, vol. 9 (Grand Rapids: Zondervan Publishing House, 1981), 157.

5. Daniel Iverson, "Spirit of the Living God," in *Hymns for the Family of God* (Nashville: Paragon Associates, Inc., 1976), hymn 155. Copyright 1935. Renewed 1963 Birdwing Music, a division of EMI Christian Music Publishing. Administered by EMI Christian Music Publishing. All rights reserved. Used by permission.

CHAPTER 11

Unless otherwise noted below, all material in this chapter is based on or quoted from "From Creation to Corruption," a sermon by Charles R. Swindoll, November 1, 1985, and chapter 11 in the *Growing Deep in the Christian Life* companion book.

1. Robert L. Thomas, ed., *New American Standard Exhaustive Concordance of the Bible* (Nashville: Holman Bible Publishers, 1981), 1501. Copyright 1981 by The Lockman Foundation. Used by permission. (www.Lockman.org)

2. Thomas, *New American Standard Exhaustive Concordance of the Bible*, 1595.

CHAPTER 12

Unless otherwise noted below, all material in this chapter is based on or quoted from "Exposing the Dark Side," a sermon by Charles R. Swindoll, November 1, 1985, and chapter 12 in the *Growing Deep in the Christian Life* companion book.

1. Mark Twain, quote accessed at http://www.quotedb.com/quotes/3088 on April 22, 2005.

2. Robert L. Thomas, ed., *New American Standard Exhaustive Concordance of the Bible* (Nashville: Holman Bible Publishers, 1981), 1604. Copyright 1981 by The Lockman Foundation. Used by permission. (www.Lockman.org)

Chapter 13

Unless otherwise noted below, all material in this chapter is based on or quoted from "Mr. Smith, Meet Your Substitute," a sermon by Charles R. Swindoll, November 10, 1985, and chapter 13 in the *Growing Deep in the Christian Life* companion book.

1. Peter Marshall, "Mr. Jones, Meet the Master," *Mr. Jones, Meet the Master*, ed. Catherine Marshall (New York: Fleming H. Revell Co., 1950), 135–136. Copyright 1950 by Fleming H. Revell, a division of Baker Publishing Group. Used by permission.

2. Robert L. Thomas, ed., *New American Standard Exhaustive Concordance of the Bible* (Nashville: Holman Bible Publishers, 1981), 1643. Copyright 1981 by The Lockman Foundation. Used by permission. (www.Lockman.org)

3. Marshall, *Mr. Jones, Meet the Master*, 30–31. Copyright 1950 by Fleming H. Revell, a division of Baker Publishing Group. Used by permission.

Chapter 14

Unless otherwise noted below, all material in this chapter is based on or quoted from "The Remedy for Our Disease," a sermon by Charles R. Swindoll, November 10, 1985, and chapter 14 in the *Growing Deep in the Christian Life* companion book.

1. John Bowring, "In the Cross of Christ I Glory," in *Hymns for the Family of God* (Nashville: Paragon Associates, Inc., 1976), hymn 251.

2. Robert L. Thomas, ed., *New American Standard Exhaustive Concordance of the Bible* (Nashville: Holman Bible Publishers, 1981), 1496. Copyright 1981 by The Lockman Foundation. Used by permission. (www.Lockman.org)

3. Thomas, *New American Standard Exhaustive Concordance of the Bible*, 1538.

4. Thomas, *New American Standard Exhaustive Concordance of the Bible*, 1687.

Chapter 15

Unless otherwise noted below, all material in this chapter is based on or quoted from "His Coming Is Sure . . . Are You?" a sermon by Charles R. Swindoll, November 17, 1985, and chapter 15 in the *Growing Deep in the Christian Life* companion book.

1. Chart adapted from *Steadfast Christianity: A Study of 2 Thessalonians* (Plano, Tex.: Charles R. Swindoll, Inc., 2002), 30.

2. Robert L. Thomas, ed., *New American Standard Exhaustive Concordance of the Bible* (Nashville: Holman Bible Publishers, 1981), 1667. Copyright 1981 by The Lockman Foundation. Used by permission. (www.Lockman.org)

CHAPTER 16

Unless otherwise noted below, all material in this chapter is based on or quoted from "Until He Returns . . . What?" a sermon by Charles R. Swindoll, November 17, 1985, and chapter 16 in the *Growing Deep in the Christian Life* companion book.

1. Robert L. Thomas, ed., *New American Standard Exhaustive Concordance of the Bible* (Nashville: Holman Bible Publishers, 1981), 1649. Copyright 1981 by The Lockman Foundation. Used by permission. (www.Lockman.org)

2. Frank E. Gaebelein, ed., "Matthew, Mark, Luke" in *The Expositor's Bible Commentary*, vol. 8 (Grand Rapids: Zondervan Publishing House, 1984), 1009. With contributors Donald A. Carson, Walter L. Liefeld, and Walter W. Wessel. Copyright © 1984 by The Zondervan Corporation. Used by permission of The Zondervan Corporation.

CHAPTER 17

Unless otherwise noted below, all material in this chapter is based on or quoted from "Visiting the <u>Real</u> Twilight Zone," a sermon by Charles R. Swindoll, November 24, 1985, and chapter 17 in the *Growing Deep in the Christian Life* companion book.

1. Rod Serling, quote accessed at http://en.wikiquote.org/wiki/The_Twilight_Zone on May 27, 2005.

2. Robert L. Thomas, ed., *New American Standard Exhaustive Concordance of the Bible* (Nashville: Holman Bible Publishers, 1981), 1586–87. Copyright 1981 by The Lockman Foundation. Used by permission. (www.Lockman.org)

3. Thomas, *New American Standard Exhaustive Concordance of the Bible*, 1655.

4. *John Doe, Disciple: Sermons for the Young in Spirit*, ed. Catherine Marshall (New York: McGraw-Hill, 1963), 219–20.

5. Bob Deffinbaugh, "A Heaven to Seek (Revelation 21:1–22:5)," quote accessed at http://www.bible.org/page.asp?page_id=1518 on June 6, 2005. Copyright 1996–2005 Biblical Studies Press. Used by permission. Related articles may be found at their Web site at www.bible.org.

CHAPTER 18

Unless otherwise noted below, all material in this chapter is based on or quoted from "An Interview with One from Beyond," a sermon by Charles R. Swindoll, November 24, 1985, and chapter 18 in the *Growing Deep in the Christian Life* companion book.

1. Robert L. Thomas, ed., *New American Standard Exhaustive Concordance of the Bible* (Nashville: Holman Bible Publishers, 1981), 1580, 1692. Copyright 1981 by The Lockman Foundation. Used by permission. (www.Lockman.org)

2. Harry A. Ironside, *Lectures on the Epistle to the Romans* (Neptune, New Jersey: Loizeaux Brothers, Inc., 1984), 71.

Chapter 19

Unless otherwise noted below, all material in this chapter is based on or quoted from "God's Body-Building Program," a sermon by Charles R. Swindoll, December 1, 1985, and chapter 19 in the *Growing Deep in the Christian Life* companion book.

1. Robert L. Thomas, ed., *New American Standard Exhaustive Concordance of the Bible* (Nashville: Holman Bible Publishers, 1981), 1646. Copyright 1981 by The Lockman Foundation. Used by permission. (www.Lockman.org)

Chapter 20

Unless otherwise noted below, all material in this chapter is based on or quoted from "Three Cheers for the Church," a sermon by Charles R. Swindoll, December 8, 1985, and chapter 20 in the *Growing Deep in the Christian Life* companion book.

1. Adapted from Joanne Weil, as told by Mike and Amy Nappa, *Bore No More!* (Loveland, Colo.: Group Publishing, 1995), 7.

2. Taken from *The Pastor's Weekly Briefing*, vol. 13, no. 16, April 22, 2005. Copyright © 2005, Focus on the Family.

3. Charles Spurgeon, *The Quotable Spurgeon* (Wheaton, Ill.: Harold Shaw Publishers, 1990), 271.

4. "How America's Faith Has Changed Since 9-11," *The Barna Update*, November 26, 2001, quote accessed at http://www.barna.org/FlexPage.aspx?Page=BarnaUpdate&BarnaUpdate ID=102. Used by permission of The Barna Group.

5. Adapted from Jay Tolson, "Forget politics. It's about the music," *U.S.News & World Report*, April 19, 2004, 72.

6. *Vine's Complete Expository Dictionary of Old and New Testament Words* (Nashville: Thomas Nelson Publishers, 1985), 50.

Chapter 21

Unless otherwise noted below, all material in this chapter is based on or quoted from "Encouragement Served Family Style," a sermon by Charles R. Swindoll, September 8, 1985, and chapter 21 in the *Growing Deep in the Christian Life* companion book.

1. Gary Larson, *The Far Side: Gallery 4* (Kansas City, Mo.: Andrews McMeel Publishing, 1993), 60.

2. Garrison Keillor, *We Are Still Married: Stories and Letters* (New York: Viking Penguin, Inc., 1989), 91–92.

3. *Merriam-Webster's Collegiate Dictionary*, 10th ed. (Springfield, Mass.: Merriam-Webster, Inc., 2000), see "discourage."

4. Scott Adams, as quoted in "My Greatest Lesson" by Anna Muoio, *Fast Company*, Issue 15, June 1998.

5. *Merriam-Webster's Collegiate Dictionary*, 10th ed., see "encourage."

6. *Theological Dictionary of the New Testament*. 1964–1976. Vols. 5–9 edited by Gerhard Friedrich. Vol. 10 compiled by Ronald Pitkin. (G. Kittel, G. W. Bromiley & G. Friedrich, ed.). Grand Rapids: William B. Eerdmans.

7. Paul Lee Tan, *Encyclopedia of 7,700 Illustrations: Signs of the Times*. (Garland, Tex.: Bible Communications, Inc., 1996). Electronic edition.

8. Adapted from Rod Cooper, "The Kiss of Encouragement," *Preaching Today*, Tape No. 141.

9. Tan, *Encyclopedia of 7,700 Illustrations: Signs of the Times*. Electronic edition.

10. *Merriam-Webster's Collegiate Dictionary*, 10th ed., see "flattery."

CHAPTER 22

Unless otherwise noted below, all material in this chapter is based on or quoted from "Worship: Let It Shine! Let It Shine!" a sermon by Charles R. Swindoll, September 22, 1985, and chapter 22 in the *Growing Deep in the Christian Life* companion book.

1. The Barna Group, "Worship," quote accessed at http://www.barna.org/FlexPage.aspx?Page= Topic&TopicID=40 on May 30, 2005. Used by permission of The Barna Group.

2. A. W. Tozer, *Whatever Happened to Worship?* (Camp Hill, Penn.: Christian Publications, Inc., 1985), 7.

3. The Barna Group, "Worship," quote accessed at http://www.barna.org/FlexPage.aspx?Page= Topic&TopicID=40 on May 30, 2005. Used by permission of The Barna Group.

4. Derek Kidner, *Psalm 73–150, A Commentary on Books III–V of the Psalms* (London: Inter-Varsity Press, 1975), 343.

5. D. R. W. Wood and I. H. Marshall, *New Bible Dictionary*. Includes index. Electronic edition of 3rd print edition. (Downers Grove, Ill.: InterVarsity Press, 1996), 1250.

6. J. Swanson, *Dictionary of Biblical Languages with Semantic Domains: Hebrew (Old Testament)* (electronic ed.). Oak Harbor, Wash.: Logos Research Systems, Inc., 2001), 2556.

7. Lawrence O. Richards, *Expository Dictionary of Bible Words* (Grand Rapids: Regency Reference Library, 1985), 640.

8. Kidner, *Psalm 73–150, A Commentary on Books III–V of the Psalms*, 346.

BOOKS FOR PROBING FURTHER

We hope you've enjoyed your spiritual journey through these eleven important areas of Christian doctrine. We pray that you've emerged from this study as a stronger, more knowledgeable, more faithful believer in Christ.

The following resources will help you continue to grow and develop in your spiritual maturity and in your love for God. We hope you'll choose several resources from the list to provide you with further encouragement and biblical principles to aid you in your spiritual walk.

Brazelton, Katie. *Pathway to Purpose for Women: Connecting Your To-Do List, Your Passions, and God's Purposes for Your Life*. Grand Rapids: Zondervan, 2005.

Foster, Richard J. *A Celebration of Discipline: The Path to Spiritual Growth*. San Francisco: HarperSanFrancisco, 1988.

Kreeft, Peter. *You Can Understand the Bible: A Practical Guide to Each Book in the Bible*. Fort Collins, Colo.: Ignatius Press, 2005.

MacArthur, John. *Faith to Grow On: Important Things You Should Know Now That You Believe*. Recommended for children ages 4–8. Nashville: Tommy Nelson, 2000.

Moore, Beth. *A Heart Like His: Seeking the Heart of God Through a Study of David*. Nashville: LifeWay Christian Resources, 1996.

———. *Believing God*. Nashville: Broadman and Holman Publishers, 2004.

———. *Breaking Free: Making Liberty in Christ a Reality in Life*. Nashville: Broadman and Holman Publishers, 2000.

———. *Praying God's Word: Breaking Free from Spiritual Strongholds*. Nashville: Broadman and Holman Publishers, 2000.

———. *When Godly People Do Ungodly Things: Arming Yourself in the Age of Seduction*. Nashville: Broadman and Holman Publishers, 2002.

Ryrie, Charles. *Basic Theology: A Popular Systematic Guide to Understanding Biblical Truth*. Chicago: Moody Publishers, 1999.

Stott, John. *Basic Christianity.* Grand Rapids: William B. Eerdmans Publishing Co., rev. ed., 1981.

Swindoll, Charles R. *So, You Want to Be Like Christ? Eight Essentials to Get You There.* Nashville: W Publishing Group, 2005.

ORDERING INFORMATION

GROWING DEEP IN THE CHRISTIAN LIFE

If you would like to order additional workbooks, purchase the audio series that accompanies this workbook, or request our product catalog, please contact the office that serves you.

United States and International Locations:

Insight for Living
Post Office Box 269000
Plano, Texas 75026-9000
1-800-772-8888, 24 hours a day, seven days a week (U.S. contacts)
International constituents may contact the U.S. office through mail queries or call 972-473-5136.
www.insight.org

Canada:

Insight for Living Ministries
Post Office Box 2510
Vancouver, BC V6B 3W7
1-800-663-7639
www.insightforliving.ca

Australia and South Pacific:

Insight for Living, Inc.
Post Office Box 1011
Bayswater, VIC 3153
AUSTRALIA
Toll-free 1300 467 444
www.insight.asn.au

NOTES

NOTES

NOTES